SOME SECRETS
OF CHRISTIAN LIVING

A Gift To
Our Partner
In Ministry

from Asbury College

Francis Asbury Publishing Company was founded in 1980 by several members of the Asbury community in Wilmore, Kentucky. Its aim was to meet the spiritual needs of that segment of the evangelical Christian public that is Wesleyan in outlook and to communicate the Wesleyan message to the larger Christian community.

In 1983 Francis Asbury Publishing Company became a part of Zondervan Publishing House. Its aim remains the spread of the Wesleyan message through the publication of popular, practical, and scholarly books.

FRANCIS ASBURY PRESS
Box 7
Wilmore, Kentucky 40390

SOME SECRETS OF CHRISTIAN LIVING

F. B. MEYER

FRANCIS ASBURY PRESS
of Zondervan Publishing House
Grand Rapids. Michigan

SOME SECRETS OF CHRISTIAN LIVING
Copyright © 1985 by the Zondervan Corporation
Grand Rapids, Michigan

FRANCIS ASBURY PRESS
is an imprint of Zondervan Publishing House
1415 Lake Drive S.E., Grand Rapids, Michigan 49506

Library of Congress Cataloging in Publication Data

F. B. (Frederick Brotherton), 1847–1929.
   Some secrets of Christian living.

   Previously published as: Steps into the blessed life.
1896.
     1. Christian life–Baptist authors. 2. Sanctification. 3. Holiness.
I. Title.

BV4501.M477   1985   248.4'861   85–14580
ISBN 0–310–38721–3

Designed by Louise Bauer
Edited by Joseph D. Allison

Printed in the United States of America

85 86 87 88 89 90 / 10 9 8 7 6 5 4 3 2 1

CONTENTS

FOREWORD:
F. B. MEYER AND THE
WESLEYANS

Frederick Brotherton Meyer (1847–1929) knew what he was doing when he refused to number himself among the theological children of the Wesleys. Yet he worked and worshiped with them and continues to influence them. His books stand on the shelves of many a Wesleyan preacher.

Meyer was a Baptist with robust Baptist convictions. He served three Baptist congregations as pastor, one of them twice. Yet he is best remembered as pastor of Christ Church, a Congregational body in the London borough of Lambeth. True enough, Christ Church had to build a baptistry suitable for adult immersions as a condition of his going there to serve; but Meyer's irenic spirit and ecumenical outlook helped others to respect their own denominational emphases as resources to be expended rather than as treasures to be defended. Meyer himself eagerly joined, supported, and often led cross-denominational ventures.

Nowhere is Meyer's ecumenical concern clearer or more typical than in his involvement in the higher life movement in Britain, Canada, and the United States. In fact, it is this involvement that has given him currency among conservative Wesleyans, including the American holiness movement.

The higher life movement, never tightly organized nor doctrinally regimented, arose in consequence of two periods of intense evangelistic work in Britain by American evangelists.

Most notable in the earlier period were Charles Finney, Asa Mahan, James Caughey, and Walter Palmer and his wife, Phoebe Worrall Palmer. All of these had come to Britain preaching and teaching the doctrine of entire sanctification. Caughey and the Palmers were convinced Methodists and held an essentially Wesleyan view of it. Mahan, a Congregationalist and an associate of Finney, had long associated closely with the Methodists, and his view was also Wesleyan at most points. Only Finney's perspective differed significantly from that of the Wesleyans.

However, a certain reluctance on the part of British Methodist officials in welcoming and endorsing the work of Caughey and the Palmers led the evangelists to extend their efforts into non-Methodist circles, where they found ready acceptance and support. And this in turn led them to adapt their message to the audience insofar as that was possible.

Their work came to remarkable fruition in the noteworthy revival of 1858. Conversions numbered in the scores of thousands. Both Established Church and Free Church took on palpable new life. But more remarkable still, believers all across Britain expressed exceptional interest in deepening and more firmly anchoring their own spiritual lives. Now the message of the American evangelists concerning entire sanctification found ready audiences.

The popularity of two books illustrates the breadth and depth of interest in that doctrine and its concomitant experience. Everywhere in the country, Asa Mahan's *Scripture Doctrine of Christian Perfection* and William E. Boardman's *Higher Christian Life* found careful and avid readers. Mahan's book was the older, having been published first in 1839, and it was more nearly Methodist. Boardman's book came out in the very year of the revival and had the greater influence. In part, its influence had to do with the fact that Boardman, a Presbyterian, had deliberately cast the doctrine of entire sanctification in terms designed to attract and nourish those whose thinking and experience had been shaped by the Reformed tradition; and this tradition, in one form or another, dominated England.

People of the Reformed tradition often found Methodist language difficult, even offensive, because it underlined the ideas of freedom and cleansing from sin. And the Methodist penchant for the terms "perfect love" and "perfection" put off many of those whose liturgies led them to confess to having sinned continually and inevitably "in thought, word, and deed." Boardman's emphasis on continuing victory over sin and on the believer's growing power to resist the inner bent to sinning held much greater allure for such people; it seemed to them more biblical and realistic than the Methodist message. Better to talk of victory over sin than freedom from it, they said. But they made no less demand than the Methodists did for a life of absolute commitment to Christlikeness and total obedience to the will of God here and now.

The fifteen years following the great revival of 1858 saw the ground prepared for an even greater harvest. Boardman's *Higher Christian Life* gained astounding popularity and was now supplemented by the clearly Wesleyan works of William Arthur and Phoebe Palmer and the more or less Reformed writings of several Anglicans, such as Edward Goulburn, and Free Churchmen, such as Richard Poole. Everywhere in Britain, prayer and study groups gathered with these authors as mentors, and time and again a twofold concern found expression: A revival must come that would include (1) the conversion of nonbelievers and (2) the deepening of the spiritual life of believers.

By late 1872, careful observers of British religious life were seeing signs that the harvest was close at hand. To cite an instance from a very telling quarter, in the first week of January 1873, the distinguished New Testament scholar F. J. A. Hort wrote his even more distinguished Cambridge colleague, B. F. Westcott, "Assuredly, the springs of life are breaking forth anew." This reflection was made upon a worship service at the university; Hort was clearly referring to revival within the Established Church. Examples of the same expectation from both Anglican and Free Church circles abound.

In fact, revival gleanings had come as early as 1871. In that year, R. Pearsall Smith and his wife, Hannah Whitall Smith, went to Britain for his health's sake. Both of them were known by a few of their British friends to be effective lay evangelists, however, and in the expectant spirit of the time it seemed unthinkable that they should be mere spectators. Moreover, Hannah Smith's *The Christian's Secret of a Happy Life,* published just a year earlier, was gaining enthusiastic readers daily. The importunings to speak and counsel and hold conferences came to be irresistible.

For about a year, Pearsall Smith contented himself with giving his testimony to having come into the experience of entire sanctification. He said the blessing had come in 1867 at the Vineland, New Jersey, campmeeting sponsored by the Methodist-led National Campmeeting Association for the Promotion of Holiness. Little by little, his insistent circle of friends got him to expand upon that testimony until he was leading evangelistic campaigns.

At the same time, Hannah Whitall Smith was testifying to the same experience, received just a bit later, with equal and even greater effect. In fact, it may be that the more nearly Reformed than Methodist perspective of the majority of Britain's Evangelicals had something to do with the somewhat more favorable acceptance they gave Hannah's witness.

The single critical difference between the two testimonies of the Smiths lay in the differing accounts of the time that the experience was received. Pearsall said that it came instantaneously. Hannah, not really contradicting but certainly thinking in more dimensions, spoke of the gradual character of her discovery of the reality of the experience.

By a series of events too complex to relate here, the Smiths found welcome in those wide evangelical circles already mentioned that had wrestled for some years with the question of sanctification, circles outside those directly under the control or influence of Methodism. And quite significantly, they gained the support of a small group of evangelical aristocracy, most particularly that of Mr. and Mrs. Cowper Temple—later Lord and Lady Mount Temple. By 1873 the

Smiths were playing major roles in the revival now sweeping the British Isles. The Moody-Sankey campaigns of 1873–1875, though not without an emphasis on "the higher life," aimed mostly at the conversion of nonbelievers. But the Smiths and others worked with the other facet of the long-time concern of British Evangelicals, the sanctification of believers.

For a number of years, believers had gathered for what had come to be called "Union Meetings for Consecration" in Ireland and England. In 1874 the Mount Temples invited those who had attended that year's meeting at Cambridge to come to Broadlands, their Hampshire estate, for an extended time of consideration of the topics of consecration and sanctification. That group met in July 1874 and in the course of their work called for another, larger such meeting as soon as would be feasible. They drew up a list of potential sponsors that included wide confessional and socio-political ranges and continental representation. As a result, the Oxford Union Meeting for the Promotion of Scriptural Holiness convened August 29, 1874, for ten days of study and meditation. It boasted an international roster of about fifteen hundred participants, including Establishment leaders, Free Churchmen, French and German pastors (whose nations had just been at war), high and low, clerics and laity. Moody, inextricably involved in a London campaign, urged all the believers who could to attend the Oxford meeting. Many of the conferees already professed enjoyment of the "higher life"; large numbers came seeking it.

The success of the Oxford meeting led to the call for another to be held May 29 to June 9, 1875, at Brighton. This time some eight thousand gathered from across Britain and the continent. All understood their purpose; they came to study and pursue "scriptural holiness." To that end, Lutherans, Anglicans, adherents of the Reformed tradition, large numbers of Methodists, and others set aside their own special theological concerns to consider the experience of sanctification. One of those who came to the experience of what he called "full sanctification" under the ministry of the Smiths and who warmly supported their work at Oxford and Brighton was the vicar of St. John's Church in the Cumberland town of Keswick, Canon T. D. Harford-Battersby. He ignited what came to be called the Keswick or Higher Life Movement by proposing a convention at his parish in late summer 1875. Its purpose would be "the full sanctification of believers."

As at Oxford and Brighton, doctrinal specialties were to be set aside at Keswick and a program of Bible study, worship, and spiritual therapy for the seeking and troubled was instituted. Pearsall Smith was to have led the first Keswick Convention, but his reputation had fallen under a cloud on its very eve, so the task fell to H. W. Webb-Peploe, with Handley C. G. Moule, Harford-Battersby, Evan Hopkins, and Robert Wilson supporting him.

Successive gatherings refined the format of the 1875 meeting, and in time the atmosphere at Keswick became more decidedly British than it had been at Oxford or Brighton—not by design, for the list of sponsors was international. By 1885, though Wesleyans had spoken there and would continue to do so occasionally, it was quite clear that the doctrine of sanctification developing at Keswick owed more and more to the pervasive Reformed perspective of those attending. The children of Calvin and those of Wesley had come to a parting of the ways on the matter. Hereafter, British Wesleyans usually supported the Southport Methodist Holiness Convention; the more or less Reformed went to Keswick.

Pearsall Smith's influence disappeared, but Hannah's remained strong among both parties. Her refusal to tie the experience of sanctification to the theological language of any single tradition made her work acceptable all around. It especially suited the "open ritual" of Keswick and the manner in which the Keswickians used the Bible and formed their theological vocabulary. They were much more inclined to work with proof texts than the Wesleyans were; and they took their language in large part from Paul's Epistle to the Romans, while the Wesleyans took theirs from the Gospels and the Johannine literature. Hannah Smith had really utilized both methods, so she came to guide both movements. But her influence was greatest among the adherents of the Higher Life Movement, the Keswickians.

William Boardman's *Higher Christian Life* had very little continuing influence among the Wesleyans but seemed to grow in popularity among the Keswickians. With *The Christian's Secret of a Happy Life,* it became a sort of theological *vade mecum* in the Higher Life Movement. It was under the influence of these works, and those of such Keswick luminaries as Webb-Peploe, Moule, and Hopkins, that F. B. Meyer sought the blessing. And it was at Keswick itself that it was given him. The Wesleyan panoply had almost no influence on him.

So in the work reprinted here, the discerning reader will find an uncompromising commitment to the experience of the "fullness of the Spirit" or "full sanctification," but in a distinctly Reformed mode. F. B. Meyer was a theologically well-educated Baptist, and in Victorian Britain such a Baptist usually held Reformed views.

Yet Meyer walks a long way with the Wesleyans. By his terms, Meyer means to refer to a second definite work of divine grace, received by faith by one already converted to Christ. He believes that this work engages the power of the Holy Spirit in such a way as to enable its recipient never to sin again by necessity.

But Meyer does say some things that no Wesleyan would say. For instance: "We certainly shall carry about with us an evil nature." And here lies the very heart of the difference between Keswickians and Wesleyans. The Wesleyan says, "It is of the very nature of the Spirit's work in entire sanctification to cleanse us from that evil nature."

Meyer is quite alert to this difference. He says, "People talk much of a clean heart; it seems to me wiser and truer to speak of the Holy Spirit as the indweller and cleanser, whose presence is purity."

Of course, a knowledgeable Wesleyan would agree that it were far better to praise the Giver than to glorify the gift, far better to attend to the relationship with the Giver than to invest any great energy in defining and defending the gift. And that Wesleyan would join Meyer in speaking of the Holy Spirit as indweller and cleanser. That Wesleyan would even say, "Yes, it is the Spirit's presence that is purity." But that Wesleyan would go on to say, "That pure presence makes the believer pure."

Perhaps the difference could be stated in this way: Meyer would say that the Holy Spirit gives power to rise victorious over all sin but not power to be pure, since God alone is truly holy and can only impute His holiness to us, not impart it to us. The Wesleyan would say that the Spirit's power cleanses us from all sin and imparts His holiness to us so that we actually are made holy as God is holy.

Both Meyer and the Wesleyan insist that the believer must surrender to God in complete consecration as the condition for receiving the gift of the fullness of the Spirit. But they would disagree concerning the purpose of that consecration. Meyer would see consecration as a necessary yielding to the Spirit in order to be empowered to live above the sin that still remains. The Wesleyan would see consecration as a necessary yielding to the Spirit in order to be cleansed of all sin and made fit for the pure love of God and neighbor. (This perspective has led some Wesleyans to believe that one can truly consecrate only *after* one has been entirely sanctified.) For Meyer, "fullness of the Spirit" means that the Spirit's power is at work in every whit of our being. For the Wesleyan, "fullness of the Spirit" means that the Spirit actually controls our whole being.

The Wesleyan would not deny the possibility of falling again into sin. But he would insist on remaining optimistic about the possibility of living "without sin, properly so called" (John Wesley).

Perhaps the difference could best be summed up by saying that Meyer would urge us to accept the gift of victory over sin; the Wesleyan would urge us to accept the gift of freedom from sin. No small difference!

No small difference, indeed. But it would violate the spirit of both Meyer and the Wesleyan to let the difference become a barrier to mutual love, respect, and helpfulness. Both believe that God's grace offers victory over sin in this life. Both believe that this is the privilege of all who believe in Christ. Both believe that it is an experience to be sought after, that it does not come simply as one more aspect of spiritual maturation.

Along these lines of agreement, F. B. Meyer has helped several generations of Wesleyans to deepen and to proclaim their faith. In fact, Meyer sounds so Wesleyan so much of the time that some Wesleyans have not seen the deep differences that are there. And that has given rise to a defensive spirit that has sometimes forbidden Meyer to help the Wesleyan. The very terms "Keswick" and "Higher Life" have been used derogatorily. This has only made Wesleyans the poorer.

Meyer is committed to holy living, both personally and in proclamation. And his clear presentation of the demands of Scripture on this matter makes him a servant well worth the Wesleyan's time. He is especially helpful at the point of the believer's desire to develop what Wesleyans call a "Christlike spirit." Meyer's is a pastoral perspective. Daily living, not doctrinal precision, occupies his mind as he writes. He knows well the joys and the testings of the sanctified.

The present book was first published in 1896 by Henry Altemus of Philadelphia under the title *Steps Into the Blessed Life*. Zondervan reissued the book in 1953 as part of the "F. B. Meyer Library," though at that time the publishing house saw fit to delete about half the text of the book, including several chapters with specific reference to Meyer's views of the higher life. This new edition restores those chapters, including "The Chambers of the King," "In the Secret of His Presence," "The Filling of the Holy Spirit," and "The Secret of Power."

It is fitting that a Wesleyan press that is itself a subdivision of a publishing house historically committed to the Reformed tradition should print a work of F. B. Meyer, a Keswickian, with a Wesleyan foreword. It is to say, "Do not gloss over the differences between Calvin's children and those of the Wesleys. But with those differences duly noted, they still may learn from each other, even at their points of doctrinal specialty."

This is especially true of F. B. Meyer and the Wesleyans. He retains considerable capacity to help his theological cousins.

PAUL MERRITT BASSETT
NAZARENE THEOLOGICAL SEMINARY

PREFACE

The apostle Paul tells us that special grace has been given to all Christians, who are "the ministers of Christ, and stewards of the mysteries of God" (1 Cor. 4:1), "even the mystery which hath been hid from ages and from generations, but now is made manifest to his saints" (Col. 1:26). Whenever, therefore, God communicates to us some secret in the divine life, unraveling what was involved or illuminating what was obscure, we are called upon to consider ourselves as the trustees or stewards of others, summoned to pass on what we have been taught.

This is what I have sought to do in these simple pages. It has been my single purpose to tell again what I have seen and handled of the Word of Life, that others may share in it. But all will be in vain apart from the demonstration of the Spirit, whose office it is to prove these things to the spirit of man, so that he may perceive them by the flash of divine revelation and spiritual insight.

Life has its mysteries, perplexities, solemn questions for us all. Probably no one can really answer them for another. The human spirit must ask its questions of God and get their solution from Him—in language not always intelligible to the intellect, though always to the heart. But each Christian may tell what God has said to him. This is what I have sought to do.

F. B. MEYER
CHRIST CHURCH
LAMBETH, ENGLAND

THE CHAMBERS
OF THE KING

THE CHAMBERS
OF THE KING

HRISTIAN experience may be compared to a suite of royal apartments, of which the first opens into the second, and that again into the third, and so on. It is of course true that believers enter on a possession of all so soon as they are born into the royal, divine household. But certain truths stand out more clearly to them at different stages of their history, and thus their successive experiences may be compared to the chambers of a palace, through which they pass to the throne room and presence chamber of their King.

And the King Himself is waiting at the threshold to act as guide. The key is in His hand, which opens and no man shuts, which shuts and no man opens. Have you entered the first of those chambers? If not, He waits to unlock the first door of all to you at this moment and to lead you forward from stage to stage until you have realized all that can be enjoyed by saintly hearts on this side of the gates of pearl. Only be sure to follow where Jesus leads the way. "Draw me, we will run after thee: the king hath brought me into his chambers . . ." (Song of Sol. 1:4). The first chamber in the king's holy palace is

THE CHAMBER OF THE NEW BIRTH.

In some cases it is preceded by a portico known as conviction for sin. But as the portico is not part of the house and all do not pass through it, we need not stay further to describe it. Over the door of this chamber are inscribed the words: "Except a man be born again, . . . he cannot enter into the kingdom of God" (John 3:3, 5).

By nature we are destitute of life, "dead in trespasses and sins" (Eph. 2:1). We need therefore, first, not a new creed but a new life. The prophet's staff is well enough to bring revival where there is life; but it is useless on the face of a dead babe. The first requisite is *life.* This is what the Holy Spirit gives us at the moment of conversion. He comes to us through some truth of the incorruptible Word of God and implants the first spark of the new life; and we who were dead, live. Thus we enter the first room in our Father's palace, where the newborn babes are welcomed and nursed and fed.

We may remember the day and place of our new birth, or we may be as ignorant of them as of the circumstances of our natural birth. But what does it matter that a man cannot recall his birthday, so long as he knows that he is alive?

As an outstretched hand has two sides—the upper, called *the back,* and the under, called *the palm*—so there are two sides of the act of entering the chamber of the new birth. Angels looking at it from the heaven side call it *being born again.* Men looking at it from the earth

24

side call it *trusting Jesus*. "But as many as received him,
to them gave he power to become the sons of God,
even to them that believe on his name: which were
born . . . of God" (John 1:12–13). If you are born
again, you will trust Jesus. And if you are trusting
Jesus, however many your doubts and fears, you are
certainly born again and have entered the palace. If you
go no further, you will be saved; but you will miss
untold blessedness.

From the chamber of birth where the newborn
ones rejoice together, realizing for the first time the
throbbing of the life of God, there is a door leading into
a second chamber, which may be called

THE CHAMBER OF ASSURANCE.

And over that door of entrance, where the King
awaits us with beckoning hand, these words are
engraved: "Beloved, now are we the sons of God"
(1 John 3:2). In many cases, of course, assurance
follows immediately on conversion, as a father's kiss
follows on his words of forgiveness to the penitent
child. But it is also true that there are some souls, truly
saved, who pass through weeks, months, and sometimes years without being sure of their standing in Jesus
or deriving any comfort from it.

True assurance comes from the work of the Holy
Spirit through the sacred Scriptures. Read the Word
looking for Christ's teaching. Think ten times of Christ
for every once of yourself. Dwell much on all refer-
ences to His finished work. Understand that you are so
truly one with Him, that you died in Him, lay with
Him in the garden tomb, rose with Him, ascended with
Him back to God, and have been already welcomed and

accepted in the Beloved (Eph. 2:5–6). Remember that His Father is your Father, that you are a son in the Son. As you dwell on these truths, opening your heart to the Holy Spirit, He will pervade your soul with a blessed conviction that you have eternal life and that you are a child, not because you feel it, but because God says so (John 3:36; Rom. 8:16–17).

The door at the farther end of this apartment leads into another chamber of the King. It is the door of consecration, leading into

THE CHAMBER OF
A SURRENDERED WILL.

Above the doorway stand the words: "From henceforth let no man trouble me: for I bear branded on my body the marks of Jesus; whose I am, and whom I serve" (Gal. 6:17 RV; cf. Acts 27:23). Consecration is giving Jesus His own. We are His by right because He bought us with His blood. *But alas, He has not had His money's worth!* He paid for all, and He has had but a fragment of our energy, time, and earnings. By an act of consecration, let us ask Him to forgive the robbery of the past. Let us profess our desire to be henceforth utterly and only for Him—His slaves, His chattels, owning no master other than Jesus Himself.

As soon as we say this, He will test our sincerity as He did the young ruler's, by asking something of us. He will lay His finger on something within us that He wants us to alter; He will call us to obey some command or abstain from some indulgence. If we instantly give up our will and way to Him, we pass the narrow doorway into the chamber of surrender, which has a southern aspect and is ever warm and radiant with

His presence, because obedience is the condition of His manifested love (John 14:23).

This doorway is very narrow, and entrance is only possible for those who will lay aside weights as well as sins. A weight is anything which, without being essentially wrong or hurtful to others, is yet a hindrance to ourselves. We may always know a weight by three signs: First, we are uneasy about it. Second, we argue for it against our conscience. Third, we go about asking people's advice, whether we may not keep it without harm. All these sins and weights must be laid aside in the strength that Jesus waits to give. Ask him to deal with them for you, that he may "make you perfect in every good work to do his will" (Heb. 13:21).

At the farther end of this apartment another door invites us to enter

THE CHAMBER OF THE FILLING OF THE SPIRIT.

Above the entrance glisten the words, "Be filled with the Spirit" (Eph. 5:18). We gladly admit that the Holy Spirit is literally in the heart of every true believer (Rom. 8:9) and that the whole work of grace in our souls is due to Him, from the first desire to be saved to the last prayer breathed on the threshold of heaven. But it is also true that a period comes in our spiritual education when we become more alive to the necessity of the Holy Spirit and seek for more of His all-pervading, heart-filling presence.

Many of us have lately been startled to find that we have been content with too little of the Holy Spirit. We have had enough water from God's throne to cover the stones in the riverbed of our lives, but not to fill its channel.

Instead of occupying all, our gracious Guest has been confined to one or two back rooms of our hearts. He is like a poor housekeeper who is sometimes put in to keep a mansion, dwelling in attic or cellar while the suites of splendid apartments are consigned to dust-sheets and cobwebs, shuttered, dismantled, and locked.

Each Christian has the Holy Spirit; but each Christian needs more and more of Him until the whole nature is filled. No, it would be truer to say that the Holy Spirit wants more and more of us. Let us ask our heavenly Father to give us of His Spirit in ever-enlarging measures; and as we ask, let us yield ourselves incessantly to His indwelling and inworking. Then let us believe that we are filled, not because we feel it, but because we are sure that God is keeping His word with us: "Ye shall not see wind, neither shall ye see rain; yet that valley shall be filled with water, that ye may drink" (2 Kings 3:17).

It is true that the filling of the Spirit involves separation—a giving up, a going apart—which is keenly bitter to the flesh. The filling of Pentecost is a baptism of fire. But there is joy amid the flames as the bonds shrivel, the limbs are free, and the Son of God walks beside.

But this chamber leads to another of exceeding blessedness:

THE CHAMBER OF
ABIDING IN CHRIST.

Around the doorway a vine is sculptured with trailing branches and pendent grapes; and entwined among the foliage these words appear: "Abide in me, and I in you" (John 15:4). The Holy Spirit never reveals

28

Himself; those who have most of His grace "wist not" what it is (Exod. 16:15). His chosen work is to reveal the Lord. We are not conscious of the Spirit, but of Him who is the Alpha and Omega of our lives. Christ's loveliness fills the soul where the Spirit is in full possession, as the odor of the ointment filled the house at Bethany (John 12:3).

Our Lord is with us all the days, but often our eyes are obscured so that we do not know Him; and if for a radiant moment we discern Him, He vanishes from our sight. There is an experience in which we not only *believe* that He is near but also *perceive* His presence by the instinct of the heart. He becomes a living, bright reality sitting by our hearth, walking beside us through the crowded streets, sailing with us across the stormy lake, standing beside the graves that hold our dead, sharing our crosses and our burdens, turning the water of common joys into the wine of holy sacraments.

Then the believer leans hard on the ever-present Lord, drawing on His fullness, appropriating His unsearchable riches, claiming from Him grace to turn every temptation into the means of increasing likeness to Christ Himself. And if the branch abide constantly in the Vine, it cannot help bearing fruit; no, the difficulty would be to keep fruit back.

We have to be concerned with the death rather than the life of our experience (Rom. 8:13). The more often we sow ourselves in the clods of daily self-denial, falling into the furrows to die, the more fruit we bear. It is by bearing about in our bodies the dying of the Lord Jesus that the life of Jesus is made manifest in our mortal flesh. Prune off every bud on the old stock, and all the energy will pass up to the rare flowers and fruits grafted there by heaven.

29

But see, the King beckons us forward to pass into

THE CHAMBER OF
VICTORY OVER SIN.

Above the door are the words: "Whosoever abid-
eth in him sinneth not" (1 John 3:6). Around the walls
hang various instruments of war (Eph. 6:13ff.) and
frescoes of the overcomers receiving the fair rewards
which the King has promised (Rev. 2–3). We must be
careful of the order in which we put these things. Many
seek victory over sin before yielding themselves entirely to God. But you can never enter this chamber
where the palm branch waves unless you have passed
through the chamber of consecration. Give yourself
wholly up to Jesus, and He will keep you.

Will you dare to say that He can hold the oceans in
the hollow of His hand, sustain the arch of heaven, and
fill the sun with light for millennia, but that He cannot
keep you from being overcome by sin or filled with the
impetuous rush of unholy passion? Can he not deliver
His saints from the sword, His darlings from the power
of the dog? Is all power given Him in heaven and on
earth, and yet He must stand paralyzed before the devils
that possess you, unable to cast them out? To ask such
questions is to answer them. "I am persuaded he is able
to keep" (2 Tim. 1:12).

We may expect to be tempted until we die. We
certainly will carry about with us an evil nature, which
would manifest itself unless kept in check by the grace
of God. But if we abide in Christ and He abide in us, if
we live under the power of the Holy Spirit, temptation
will excite no fascination in us but, on the contrary,
horror. The least stirring of our self-life will be

instantly noticed and met by the Name and Blood and Spirit of Jesus. The tides of His purity and life will flow so strongly over our being as to sweep away any black drops of ink oozing upwards from the sand.

However, you must irrevocably shut the back door, as well as the front door, against sin. You must not dally with it as being possible in any form. You must see that you are shut up to saintliness by the purpose of God (Rom. 8:29). You must definitely and forever elect the cross as the destiny of your self-life. You will find that Christ will save you from all that you dare to trust Him with. Remember God's promise to Joshua: "Every place that the sole of your foot shall tread upon, that have I given unto you" (Josh. 1:3).

And His work within us is most perfect when it is least apparent, when the flesh is kept so utterly in abeyance that we begin to think it has been altogether extracted.

Yet another door, at the far end of this chamber, summons us to advance to

THE CHAMBER OF HEART REST.

The King Himself spoke its motto text: "Take my yoke upon you, and learn of me . . . and ye shall find rest unto your souls" (Matt. 11:29). Here soft strains float on the air, and the peace of God stands sentry against intruding care. Of course the soul learned something of rest at the very outset of its pilgrimage; but these words of the Master indicate that there are at least two kinds of rest. The rest of forgiveness passes into the rest of surrender and satisfaction.

We lay our worries and cares where once we laid only our sins. We lose the tumultuous fever and haste of earlier days. We become oblivious to praise on the one hand and censure on the other. Our soul is poised on God, is satisfied with God, seeks nothing outside God, regards all things from the standpoint of eternity and of God. The life loses the babble of its earlier course and sweeps onward to the ocean, from which it derived its being. The very face tells the tale of the sweet, still life within, which is attuned to the everlasting chime of the land where storms come not, nor conflict, nor alarm.

Some say that the door at the end of this chamber leads into

THE CHAMBER OF FELLOWSHIP IN CHRIST'S SUFFERINGS.

It may be so. All along the Christian's course there is a great and growing love for the world for which Christ died. There are times when that love amounts almost to an agony of compassion and desire; and there come sufferings caused by the thorn crown, the sneer, the mockery, the cross, the spear, the baptism of blood and tears. All these fall to the lot of the followers of the King; and perhaps they come most plentifully to the saintliest, those who are most like the Lord.

But it is certain that those who suffer thus are also the ones who reign. Their sufferings are not for a moment to be compared to the glory revealed in their lives. And out of their bitter griefs, sweetened by the Cross, gush water springs to refresh the weary children of God like the waters of the Exodus (Exod. 15:25).

Beyond all these, and separated from them by a very slight interval, are

THE MANSIONS OF
THE FATHER'S HOUSE,

into which the King will lead us presently. Here we will pass through chamber after chamber of delight, stretch after stretch of golden glory, until this human nature (which is but as an infant's) has developed to the measure of the stature of our full growth, unto the likeness of the Son of God.

To which of the King's chambers have you attained? Do not linger inside the first chamber, but press on and forward. If any door seems locked, knock, and it shall be opened unto you. Never consider that you have fully attained or are already perfect, but follow on to apprehend all that for which Jesus Christ apprehended you.

IN THE SECRET
OF HIS PRESENCE

IN THE SECRET
OF HIS PRESENCE

I N one sense God is always near us. He is not an absentee, needing to be brought down from the heavens or up from the deep. He is near at hand. His being pervades all being. Every world that floats like an islet in the ocean of space is filled with signs of His presence, just as the home of your friend is littered with the many evidences of his residence, by which you know that he lives there. Every crocus pushing through the dark mold, every firefly in the forest, every bird that springs up from its nest before your feet, everything that is—*all* are as full of God's presence as the bush that burned with His fire, before which Moses bared his feet in acknowledgment that God was there.

REALIZING GOD'S PRESENCE

But we do not always realize He is there. We often pass hours, days, and weeks without a sense of His presence. We sometimes engage in seasons of prayer, we go to and fro from His house where the ladder of communion rests, and still He seems like a shadow, a name, a tradition, a dream of days gone by.

"Oh that I knew where I might find him! that I might come even to his seat! . . . Behold, I go forward, but he is not there; and backward, but I cannot perceive him: on the left hand, where he doth work, but I cannot behold him; he hideth himself on the right hand, that I cannot see him" (Job 23:3, 8–9).

How different is this failure to realize the presence of God to the blessed experience of His nearness realized by some. Brother Lawrence, the simple-minded cook, tells us that for more than sixty years he never lost the sense of the presence of God but was as conscious of it while performing the duties of his humble office as when partaking of the Holy Supper.

John Howe, on the blank page of his Bible, made this record in Latin: "This very morning I awoke out of a most ravishing and delightful dream, when a wonderful and copious stream of celestial rays, from the lofty throne of the divine majesty, seemed to dart into my open and expanded breast. I have often since reflected on that very signal pledge of special divine favor, and have with repeated fresh pleasure tasted the delights thereof." Another experience is recorded thus: "Suddenly there came on my soul something I had never known before. It was as if someone infinite and almighty, knowing everything, full of the deepest, tenderest interest in myself, made known to me that He loved me. My eye saw no one, but I knew assuredly that the One whom I knew not, and had never met, had met me for the first time, and made known to me that we were together."

Are not these experiences, so blessed and inspiring, similar to that of the author of the longest (and in some respects the most sublime) psalm in the Psalter? He had been beating out the golden ore of thought through successive paragraphs of marvelous power and beauty, when suddenly he seemed to become conscious that the Lord, of whom he had been speaking, had drawn near and was bending over him. The sense of the presence of God was borne in upon his inner consciousness and, lifting up a face on which reverence and ecstasy met and mingled, he cried, "Thou art near, O Lord" (Ps. 119:151).

THE BLESSINGS OF
REALIZING GOD'S PRESENCE

If only such an experience of the nearness of God were always ours, enwrapping us as air or light! If only we could feel, as the great apostle put it on Mars' Hill, that God is not far away but the element in which we have our being (Acts 17:27–28), as sea flowers in deep, still lagoons! Then we should understand what David meant when he spoke about dwelling in the house of the Lord all the days of his life (Ps. 23), beholding God's beauty, inquiring in his temple, and hidden in the secret of his pavilion (Ps. 27). Then, too, we should acquire the blessed secret of *peace, purity,* and *power.*

1. *In the secret of His presence there is peace.* "In the world ye shall have tribulation," our Master said (John 16:33). "But now in Christ Jesus ye who sometimes were far off are made nigh by the blood of Christ. For he is our peace" (Eph. 2:13–14). It is said that a certain insect has the power of surrounding itself with a film of air in which it drops into the midst of muddy, stagnant

pools and remains unhurt. The believer is conscious that he is also enclosed in the invisible film of the divine presence, as a far-traveled letter in the envelope that protects it from hurt and soil.

"They draw nigh that follow after mischief" (Ps. 119:150), but God is nearer than the nearest, and I dwell in the inner ring of His presence. The mountains round about me are filled with the horses and chariots of His protection; no weapon that is formed against me can prosper, for it can reach me only through Him and, touching Him, will glance harmlessly aside. To be in God is to be in a well-fitted house when the storm has slipped from its leash; or in a sanctuary, the doors of which shut out the pursuer.

2. *In the secret of His presence there is purity.* The mere vision of snow-capped Alps, seen from across Lake Geneva, so elevates the rapt and wistful soul as to abash all evil things that would thrust themselves upon the inner life. The presence of a little child with its guileless purity has been known to disarm passion, as a beam of light falling in a reptile-haunted cave scatters the slimy snakes. And what shall not God's presence do for me, if I acquire a perpetual sense of it and live in its secret place? Surely, in the heart of that fire, black cinder though I be, I shall be kept pure and glowing and intense!

3. *In the secret of His presence there is power.* My cry day and night is for power—spiritual power. Not the power of intellect, oratory, or human might; these cannot avail to vanquish the serried ranks of evil.

Lord, You say truly that "it is not by might, nor power" that the battle is won (Zech. 4:6). Yet human souls that touch You become magnetized and charged with a spiritual force which the world can neither gainsay nor resist. Oh, let me touch You! Let me dwell in unbroken contact with You, so that successive tides of divine energy may pass out of You into and through my emptied and eager spirit, flowing but never ebbing, and lifting me into a life of blessed ministry that will make deserts like the garden of the Lord!

THE ESSENTIALS FOR REALIZING GOD'S PRESENCE

But how shall we get and keep this sense of God's nearness? Must we go back to Bethel and its pillar of stone, where even Jacob said, "Surely the LORD is in this place" (Gen. 28:16)? We might have stood beside him with unanointed eye and seen no ladder, heard no voice! Yet the patriarch would discover God in the bare moorlands of our lives, trodden by us without reverence or joy.

Must we travel to the mouth of the cave in whose shadow Elijah stood, thrilled by the music of the still small voice, sweeter by contrast with the thunder and the storm (1 Kings 19:9ff.)? Alas! We might have stood beside him, unconscious of that glorious presence, while Elijah, if living now, would discern it in the whisper of the wind, the babbling of babes, the rhythm of heart throbs.

If we had stationed ourselves in our present state beside the apostle Paul when he was caught into the third heaven (2 Cor. 12:2), we should probably have seen nothing but a tentmaker's shop or a dingy room in a hired lodging. We would stand in the dark while he was in transports. Yet he would discern, were he to live again, angels on our steamships, visions in our temples, and doors opening into heaven amid the tempered glories of our more somber skies.

In point of fact, we carry everywhere our circumference of light or dark. God is as much in the world as He was when Moses communed with Him face to face and when Enoch walked with Him. He is as willing to be a living, bright, glorious reality to us as to them. But the fault is with us. Our eyes are unanointed because our hearts are not right. The pure in heart still see God. To those who love Him and do His commandments, He still manifests Himself as He does not to the world. Let us cease to blame our times; let us blame ourselves. We are degenerate, not they.

What, then, is that temper of soul that most readily perceives the presence and nearness of God? Let us endeavor to learn the blessed secret of abiding ever in the secret of His presence and of being hidden in His pavilion (Ps. 31:20).

Remember at the outset that neither you nor any of our race can have this glad consciousness of the presence of God except through Jesus. None knows the Father but the Son and those to whom the Son reveals Him; and none comes to the Father but by Him. Apart from Jesus, the presence of God is an object of terror, from which devils hide themselves in hell and sinners weave aprons of shame or hide among the trees. But in Him all barriers are broken down, all veils rent, all clouds dispersed, and the weakest believer may live where Moses sojourned in the midst of the fire, before whose consuming flames no impurity can stand.

What part of the Lord's work is most closely connected with this blessed sense of the presence of God? It is through the blood of His cross that sinners are brought near to God. For in His death He not only revealed the tender love of God but also put away our sins and wove for us those garments of stainless beauty in which we are gladly welcomed into the inner chamber of the King. Remember that God said, "I will commune with thee from above the mercy seat" (Exod. 25:22). That golden slab, on which Aaron sprinkled blood whenever he entered the Most Holy Place, was a type of Jesus; He is the true mercy seat. And it is when you enter into deepest fellowship with Him in His death, when you live most constantly in the spirit of His memorial supper, that you will realize most deeply His nearness. Now, as at Emmaus, He loves to make Himself known in the breaking of bread (Luke 24:35).

"And is that all?" you ask. "For I have heard this many times and still fail to live in the secret place as I would."

Exactly so. Therefore, to do for us what no effort of ours could do, our Lord has received of His Father the promise of the Holy Spirit, that He should bring into our hearts the very presence of God.

Understand that since you are Christ's, the blessed Comforter is yours. He is within you as He was within your Lord. And in proportion as you live in the Spirit, walk in the Spirit, and open your entire nature to Him, you will find yourself becoming His presence chamber, irradiated with the light of His glory. As you realize that He is in you, you will realize that you are ever in Him. Thus, the apostle John wrote, "Hereby know we that we dwell in him, and he in us, because he hath given us of his Spirit" (1 John 4:13).

"All this I know," you may respond, "and yet I fail to realize this marvelous fact of the indwelling of the Spirit in me. How then can I ever realize my indwelling in Him?"

It is because your life is so hurried. You do not

take time enough for meditation and prayer. The Spirit of God within you and the presence of God around you cannot be discerned while the senses are occupied with pleasure, or while the pulse beats quickly, or while the brain is filled with the tread of many hurrying thoughts. It is when water stands still that it becomes pellucid and reveals the pebbly beach below. Be still and know that God is within and around you.

In the hush of the soul the unseen becomes visible and the eternal real. The eye dazzled by the sun cannot detect the beauties of the sky until it has had time to rid itself of the glare. Therefore, let no day pass without its season of silent waiting before God.

OTHER CONDITIONS FOR
REALIZING GOD'S PRESENCE

You ask, "Are there any other conditions that I should fulfill so that I may abide in the secret of His presence?"

1. *Be "pure in heart"* (Matt. 5:8). Every permitted sin encrusts the windows of the soul with thicker layers of grime, obscuring your vision of God. But every victory over impurity and selfishness clears the spiritual vision and there fall from the eyes, as it had been, scales. In the power of the Holy Spirit deny self, give no quarter to sin, resist the Devil, and you "shall see God."

The unholy soul could not see God, even though it were set down in the midst of heaven. But holy souls see God amid the commonplaces of earth and find everywhere an open vision of His beauty. Such people could not be nearer God, though they stood by the sea of glass (Rev. 15:2). Their only advantage there would be that the veil of their mortal and sinful natures having been rent, their vision would be more direct and more perfect.

2. *Keep Christ's commandments.* Let there be not one jot or tittle of His Word unrecognized and unkept. "He that hath my commandments, and keepeth them, he it is that loveth me: and he that loveth me shall be loved of my Father, and I will love him, and will manifest myself to him" (John 14:21). Moses, the faithful servant of God, was also the companion of God. He spoke with God "face to face, as a man speaketh unto his friend" (Exod. 33:11).

3. *Continue in the spirit of prayer.* Sometimes the vision of God will tarry to test the earnestness and steadfastness of your desire. At other times it will come as the dawn steals over the sky and, quite by surprise, you find yourself conscious that He is near. He was ever accustomed to glide unheralded into the midst of His disciples through unopened doors. As the psalmist said to him, "Thy footsteps are not known" (Ps. 77:19).

At such times we may truly say with St. Bernard: "He entered not by the eyes, for His presence was not marked by color; nor by the ears, for there was no sound; nor by the breath, for He mingled not with the air; nor by the touch, for He was impalpable. You ask, then, how I knew that He was present. Because He was a quickening power. As soon as He entered, He awoke my slumbering soul; He moved and pierced my heart, which before was strange, stony, hard and sick, so that my soul could bless the Lord, and all that is within me praised His holy name."

4. *Cultivate the habit of speaking aloud to God.* Not at all times, perhaps, because our desires are often too

sacred or deep to be put into words. But it is well to acquire the habit of speaking to God as to a present friend while sitting in the house or walking by the way. Seek the habit of talking things over with God—your letters, your plans, your hopes, your mistakes, your sorrows and sins. Things look very differently when brought into the calm light of His presence. One cannot talk long with God aloud without feeling that He is near.

5. *Meditate much upon the Word.* This is the garden where the Lord God walks, the temple where He dwells, the presence chamber where He holds court and is found by those who seek Him. It is through the written Word that we feed upon the living Word. And Jesus said: "He that eateth my flesh, and drinketh my blood, dwelleth in me, and I in him" (John 6:56).

6. *Be diligent in Christian work.* The place of prayer is indeed the place of His manifested presence. But that presence would fade from it were we to linger there after the bell of duty had rung for us below. We will ever meet it as we go about our necessary work: "LORD, who shall abide in thy tabernacle? who shall dwell in thy holy hill? He that walketh uprightly, and worketh righteousness . . ." (Ps. 15:1–2). As we go forth to our daily tasks the Angel of His presence comes to greet us and turns to go at our side. "Go ye," said the Master. "And, lo, I am with you alway" (Matt. 28:19–20). Not only in temple courts, or in sequestered glens, or in sick rooms; but in the round of daily duty, in the commonplaces of life, on the dead levels of existence, we may be ever in the secret of His presence and be able to say with Elijah before Ahab, and Gabriel to Zacharias, that we stand in the presence of God (1 Kings 17:1; Luke 1:19).

Let us cultivate the habit of recognizing the presence of God. "Blessed is the man whom thou choosest, and causest to approach unto thee, that he may dwell in thy courts" (Ps. 65:4a). There is no life like this, to feel that God is with us; that He never leads us through a place too narrow for Him to pass as well; that we can never be lonely again, never for a single moment; that we are beset by Him behind and before, and covered by His hand; that He could not be nearer to us, even if we were in heaven itself; to have Him as friend, and referee, and counselor, and guide; to realize that there is never to be a Jericho in our lives without the presence of the Captain of the Lord's host with those invisible but mighty legions, before whose charge all walls must fall down. Little wonder that the saints of old waxed valiant in fight as they heard Him say: "I will be with thee: I will not fail thee, nor forsake thee" (Josh. 1:5). Begone, fear and sorrow and dread of the dark valley! "Thou shalt hide [me] in the secret of thy presence from the pride of man; thou shalt keep [me] secretly in a pavilion from the strife of tongues" (Ps. 31:20).

THE SECRET OF CHRIST'S INDWELLING

THE SECRET OF CHRIST'S INDWELLING

T IS proper that the largest church in London, the greatest Gentile city in the Old World, should be dedicated to the apostle Paul. Gentiles are under a great obligation to him as the Apostle to the Gentiles. It is to him that we owe, under the Spirit of God, the unveiling of two great mysteries that specially touch us as Gentiles.

The *first* of these, glorious as it is, we cannot now discuss, though it wrought a revolution when first preached and maintained by Paul in the face of the most strenuous opposition. Before that time, Gentiles were expected to become Jews before they could be Christians; they had to pass through the synagogue to the church. But Paul showed that Gentiles stood on the same level as Jews with respect to the privileges of the gospel. They were equal heirs and members of the body of Christ, equal partakers of the promise in Christ Jesus through the gospel (Eph. 3:6).

The *second* mystery, however, well deserves our

further thought. If only it could be realized by the children of God, they would begin to live after so divine a fashion as to still the enemy and avenger, repeating in some small measure the life of Jesus on the earth. This mystery is *that the Lord Jesus is willing to dwell within the Gentile heart.*

That He should dwell in the heart of a child of Abraham was deemed a marvelous act of condescension; but that He should find a home in the heart of a Gentile was incredible. This mistake was dissipated before the radiant revelation of truth made to him who, in his own judgment, was not fit to be called an apostle because he had persecuted the church of God. God was pleased to make known through him "the riches of the glory of this mystery among the Gentiles; which is *Christ in you,* the hope of glory" (Col. 1:27, italics added).

"Master, where dwellest thou?" they asked of old (John 1:38). And in reply, Jesus led them from the crowded Jordan bank to the tiny hut of woven reeds where He temporarily lodged. But if we address the same question to Him now, He will point, not to the high and lofty dome of heaven, not to the splendid structure of stone or marble, but to the happy spirit that loves, trusts, and obeys Him. "Behold," says He, "I stand at the door and knock: if any man hear my voice, and open the door, I will come in to him" (Rev. 3:20). "We will come unto him," He said, including His Father with Himself, "and make our abode with him" (John 14:23). He promised to be within each believer as a tenant in a house, as sap in the branch, as life blood and life energy in each member (however feeble) of the body.

THE MYSTERY

Christ is in the believer. He indwells the heart by faith, as the sun indwells the lowliest flowers that unfurl their petals and bare their hearts to His beams. Christ lives within us, not because we are good, not because we are trying to be wholehearted in our consecration, not because we keep Him by the tenacity of our love. He lives within us simply because we believe and, in believing, have thrown open all the doors and windows of our nature. So He has come in.

He probably came in so quietly that we failed to detect His entrance. There was no footfall along the passage; the chime of the golden bells at the foot of His priestly robe did not betray Him. He stole in as if He were on the wing of the morning or like the noise-lessness with which nature arises from her winter's sleep and arrays herself in the robes that her Creator has prepared for her. This is the way of Christ. He does not strive, nor cry, nor cause His voice to be heard. His tread is so light that it does not break the bruised reed; His breath so soft that it can revive dying sparks. Do not be surprised, therefore, if you cannot tell the day or the hour when the Son of Man came to dwell within you. Only know that He has come. "Know ye not your own selves, how that Jesus Christ is in you? except ye be reprobates?" (2 Cor. 13:5).

1 *It is very wonderful.* The heavens, with all their light and glory, alone seem worthy of Him. But even there He is not more at home than He is with the humble and contrite spirit that simply trusts in Him. In His earthly life He said that the Father dwelled in Him so really that the words He spoke and the works He did were not His own, but His Father's. And He desires to

be in us as His Father was in Him, so that the outgoings of our life may be channels through which He, hidden within, may pour Himself forth upon men.

2. *It is not generally recognized.* It is not, though that does not disprove it. We fail to recognize many things in ourselves and in nature that are nevertheless true. But there is a reason why many whose natures are certainly the temple of Christ remain ignorant of the presence of the wonderful tenant who sojourns within. *He dwells so deep*—below the life of the body, which is as the curtain of the tent; below the life of the soul, where thought and feeling, judgment and imagination, hope and love go to and fro, ministering as white-stoled priests in the Holy Place; below the play of light and shade, resolution and will, memory and hope, the perpetual ebb and flow of the tides of self-consciousness—there, in the person of the Holy Spirit, Christ dwells, as of old the Shekinah glory dwelled in the Most Holy Place, closely shrouded from the view of man.

It is comparatively seldom that we go into these deeper departments of our being. We are content to live the superficial life of sense. We eat, we drink, we sleep. We give ourselves to enjoy the lust of the flesh, the lust of the eyes, and the pride of life. We fulfill the desires of the flesh and of the mind. Or we abandon ourselves to the pursuit of knowledge and culture, of science and art; we reason, speculate, and argue. We make short forays into the realm of morals, that sense of right and wrong that is part of the make-up of men. But we have too slight an acquaintance with the deeper and more mysterious chamber of the spirit. Now this is why the majority of believers are so insensible of their divine and wonderful resident, who makes the regenerated spirit His abode.

3. *It is to be accepted by faith.* We repeat here our constant mistake about the things of God. We try to feel them. If we feel them, we believe them; otherwise we take no account of them. We reverse the divine order. We say, "Feeling . . . faith . . . fact." God says, "Fact . . . faith . . . feeling." With him, feeling is of small account. He only asks us to be willing to accept His own Word and cling to it because He has spoken it, in entire disregard of what we may feel.

In Scripture I am distinctly told that Christ, though He is on the throne in His ascended glory, is also within me by the Holy Spirit. I confess I do not feel Him there. Often amid the assault of temptation or the fury of the storm that sweeps over the surface of my nature, I cannot detect His form or hear Him say, "It is I." But I dare to believe He is there: not without me, but within; not as a transient sojourner for a night, but as a perpetual resident; not altered by my changes from earnestness to lethargy, from the summer of love to the winter of despondency, but always and unchangeably the same. And I say again and again, "Jesus, You are here. I am not worthy that You should abide under my roof; but You have come. Assert Yourself. Put down all rule, and authority, and power. Come out of Your secret chamber and possess all that is within me, that it may bless Your holy name."

Catherine of Siena once spent three days in a solitary retreat, praying for a greater fullness and joy of the divine presence. Instead of this, it seemed as though legions of wicked spirits assailed her with blasphemous thoughts and evil suggestions.

At length, a great light appeared to descend from above. The devils fled, and the Lord Jesus conversed with her. Catherine asked him, "Lord, where were You when my heart was so tormented?"

"I was in your heart," He answered.

"O Lord, You are everlasting truth," she replied, "and I humbly bow before Your word. But how can I believe that You were in my heart when it was filled with such detestable thoughts?"

"Did these thoughts give you pleasure or pain?" He asked.

"An exceeding pain and sadness," was her reply.

To which the Lord said, "You were in woe and sadness because I was in the midst of your heart. My presence rendered those thoughts insupportable to you. When the period I had determined for the duration of the combat had elapsed, I sent forth the beams of My light, and the shades of hell were dispelled, because they cannot resist that light."

THE GLORY OF THIS MYSTERY

When God's secrets break open, they do so in glory. The wealth of the root hidden in the ground is revealed in the hues of orchid or the scent of rose. The hidden beauty of a beam of light is unraveled in the sevenfold color of the rainbow. The swarming, infinitesimal life of the South Seas breaks into waves of phosphorescence when cleft by the keel of the ship. And whenever the unseen world has revealed itself to mortal eyes, it has been in glory. It was especially so at the Transfiguration, when the Lord's nature broke from the strong restraint within which he confined it, and revealed itself to the eye of man. "His face did shine as the sun, and his raiment was white as the light" (Matt. 17:2).

So when we accept the fact of His existence within us, deeper than our own, and make it an aim of life to draw on it and develop it, we will be conscious of a glory transfiguring our lives and irradiating ordinary things, as if to make earth with its commonest engagements like the vestibule of heaven.

The wife of Jonathan Edwards had been the subject of great fluctuations in religious experience and frequent depression, till she came to the point of renouncing the world and yielding herself up to be possessed by these mighty truths. But as soon as she did, a marvelous change took place. She began to experience a constant, uninterrupted rest; sweet peace and serenity of soul; a continual rejoicing in all the works of God's hands, whether of nature or of daily providence; a wonderful access to God by prayer, as if seeing Him and immediately conversing with Him; all tears wiped away; all former troubles and sorrows of life forgotten (excepting grief for past sins and for the dishonor done to Christ in the world); a daily sensible doing and suffering everything for God; and doing all with a continual uninterrupted cheerfulness, peace, and joy.

Such glory—the certain pledge of the glory to be revealed when Christ returns—is within reach of each reader of these lines, who will dare day by day to reckon that Christ lives within. It is within the reach of every Christian who will be content to die to the energies and promptings of the self-life, that so there may be room for the Christ life to reveal itself. "I am crucified," said the greatest human teacher of this divine art; ". . . Christ liveth in me: . . . I live by the faith of the Son of God" (Gal. 2:20).

THE RICHES OF
THE GLORY OF THIS MYSTERY

When this mystery or secret of the divine life in man is apprehended and made use of, it gives great wealth to life. If all the treasures of wisdom, knowledge, power, and grace reside in Jesus, and He is become the cherished and honored resident of our nature, it is clear that we also must be greatly enriched. It is like a poor man having a millionaire friend come to live with him.

1. *There are riches of patience.* Life is not easy for any of us. No branch escapes the pruning knife, no jewel the wheel, no child the rod. People tyrannize over us and vex us almost beyond endurance. Circumstances strain us till the chords of our hearts threaten to snap. Our nervous systems are overtaxed by the rush and competition of our times. Indeed we have need of patience!

Having Christ within us means never to relax the self-watch; never to indulge in unkind or thoughtless criticism of others; never to utter the hasty word or permit the sharp retort; never to complain, except to God; never to permit hard and distrustful thoughts to lodge within the soul. It permits us to be always more thoughtful of others than of self; to detect the one blue spot in the clouded sky; to be on the alert to find an excuse for those who are forward and awkward; to suffer the aches, pains, privations, and trials of life sweetly, submissively, and trustfully; to drink the bitter cup with the eye fixed on the Father's face, without a murmur or complaint. All of this requires a patience that mere stoicism could never give.

We cannot live such a life till we have learned to

avail ourselves of the riches of the indwelling Christ. The beloved apostle John speaks of being a partaker of the patience that is in Jesus (Rev. 1:9). So may we be. That calm, unmurmuring, unreviling patience, which made the Lamb of God dumb before His shearers, is ours. Robert Hall was once overheard saying, amid the heat of an argument, "Calm me, O Lamb of God!" But we may go further and say, "Lord Jesus, let Your patience arise in me as a spring of fresh water in a briny sea."

2. *There are riches of grace.* Alone among the great cities of the world, Jerusalem had no river. But the glorious Lord was in the midst of her, and He became a place of broad rivers and streams, supplying from Himself all that rivers gave to other cities, at the foot of whose walls the welcome waters lapped (Isa. 33:21).

This is a picture of what we have when we dare to reckon the indwelling of "our glorious Lord" as king, lawgiver, and savior. He makes all grace to abound toward us, so that we have a sufficiency for all emergencies and can abound in every good work. In His strength, ever rising up within us, we are able to do as much as those who are endowed with the greatest mental and natural gifts, and we escape the temptations to vainglory and pride by which they are beset.

The grace of purity and self-control, of fervent prayer and understanding in the Scriptures, of love for men and zeal for God, of lowliness and meekness, of gentleness and goodness—all of these are in Christ. And if Christ is in us, all of them are ours also. Oh, that we would dare to believe it and draw on it, letting down the pitcher of faith into the deep well of Christ's indwelling, which has been opened within us by the Holy Spirit!

OUR PARTICIPATION
IN THIS MYSTERY

It is impossible, in these brief pages, to elaborate further this wonderful thought. But if only we would meet every call, difficulty, and trial—*not* saying as we so often do, "I shall never be able to go through it," but saying, "I cannot; but Christ is in me, and He can"— then we should find that all trials were intended to reveal and unfold the wealth hidden within us, until Christ was literally formed within us and His life manifested in our mortal body (2 Cor. 4:10).

1. *Be still each day for a short time, sitting before God in meditation, and ask the Holy Spirit to reveal to you the truth of Christ's indwelling.* Ask God to make known to you the riches of the glory of this mystery (Col. 1:27).

2. *Reverence your nature as the temple of the indwelling Lord.* As the Eastern worshiper bares his feet, and the Westerner his head, on entering the precincts of a temple, so be very careful of anything that would defile your body or soil your soul. No beasts must herd in your temple courts; get Christ to drive them out. "Know ye not that ye are the temple of God, and that the Spirit of God dwelleth in you? . . . The temple of God is holy, which temple ye are" (1 Cor. 3:16–17).

3. *Hate your own life.* "If any man . . . hate not . . . his own life," said the Lord, ". . . he cannot be my disciple" (Luke 14:26). And the word translated "life" literally means *soul,* the seat and center of the self-life with its restless energies and activities, its choices and decisions, its ceaseless strivings at independence and leadership. This is the greatest hindrance to our enjoyment of the indwelling Christ. If we will acquire the habit of saying no, not only to our bad but to our good

self; if we will daily deliver ourselves up to death for Jesus' sake; if we will take up our cross and follow the Master, though it be to His grave, then we will become increasingly conscious of being possessed by a richer, deeper, more divine life than our own.

4. *Dwell deep.* There is a depth of life in each Christian soul that is too seldom brought into use. We live too much on the surface and know but little of the depth that lies beneath.

The story is told of a slave pining for freedom, who discovered a mine from which he brought enough ore to purchase his freedom. Then it seemed exhausted, and he was threatened with starvation. But returning to the mine, he suddenly became aware of the glistening of metal in a different direction from that in which he had been working. He again took up pickax and spade and followed the new lode, which led him deep into the earth but made him rich.

Thus, in the depths of the spirit's life, where Jesus lives by the Holy Spirit, there are resources that would enrich our existence with a new energy, a fuller life, a more intense enthusiasm. They are nominally ours by possession; they may become practically ours by use and by dwelling deep in Christ.

THE FILLING OF
THE HOLY SPIRIT

THE FILLING OF
THE HOLY SPIRIT

OMING down to Ephesus, the apostle Paul, as was his custom, sought for any Christians that might be gathered within that vast center of heathenism. His search was finally rewarded by the discovery of twelve men, meeting probably in some obscure room and exercising no influence on the vast idolatrous city out of which the grace of God had drawn them. His first question was very searching. Without preliminaries he went to the point. Convinced that there must be some reason why they did not exercise a greater power on the populations around them, he set himself to probe the cause; and shrewdly guessed it in the searching inquiry: "Did ye receive the Holy Spirit when ye believed?" (Acts 19:2 RV).

THE EXPERIENCE OF THE FILLING

The apostle surely did not mean to ask whether they had received the special gifts of the Spirit; their reply at least does not indicate that they so understood him. He wanted only to learn whether they had received that filling of the Holy Spirit, which was the main feature of Pentecost (Acts 2:4; 6:3; 13:52).

"Received we the Holy Spirit when we believed!" might have been the reply of the startled men. "How could we have faith, except it were given us by the Holy Spirit?"

"Granted," would the apostle answer. "No man can call Jesus Lord except by the Holy Spirit. Certainly the Holy Spirit has been at work within you, else ye were none of Christ's. But there is an experience altogether beyond and above that initial step by which the Holy Spirit first reveals sin and Christ, and it is for lack of this that your testimony is so inoperative and your lives so destitute of fire."

And as we look back upon this episode across the centuries, we are convinced that it suggests the reason why so many Christians around us acknowledge their religion a failure, while the world mocks at their inability to exorcise the devils that possess it.

It is, of course, true that the Holy Spirit is the sole agent in conversion, becoming the occupant of the temple, which is presented to Him by the nature of man (1 Cor. 6:19). And it is equally clear that the Holy Spirit as a person enters the newly regenerated heart. But there is a vast difference between having the Holy Spirit and being filled by Him. In the one case, He may be compared to a mighty man that cannot save, relegated to an obscure corner of the heart while the larger part of the nature is excluded from His gracious influences. In the other, He is a welcome guest to whom every part of the being is thrown open and who pervades it with the freedom of the balmy air of summer, sweeping through open windows, breathing through long corridors, and carrying into further recesses the fragrance of a thousand flowers.

There are a great many Christians who undoubtedly received the Holy Spirit at the earliest moment of faith; indeed, their faith is the result of His work. But they have never gone farther. They have never yielded their whole nature to His indwelling. They have had no further experience of His Pentecostal filling.

It is not difficult to reveal this contrast by analogies drawn from the Word of God. May we not reverently say that the ministry of our blessed Lord Himself owed much of its marvelous power to that moment when, although filled with the Holy Spirit from His birth, He was afresh anointed at the waters of baptism? With marked emphasis it is said He was filled with the Spirit (Luke 4:1), returned in the power of the Spirit to Galilee (v. 14), and stood up in the synagogue of His native town, claiming the ancient prophecy and declaring that the Spirit of God was upon Him (v. 18). His wondrous words and works are directly traced to the marvelous operation of the Holy Spirit upon His human life (Acts 10:38).

Remember also the vast alteration that came over the apostles and other followers of Jesus Christ on the Day of Pentecost and after! Before that day, they cowered like sheep; when it came, they stood like lions at bay. Before it, their bosoms heaved with tumultuous passions of rivalry and suspicion and desire for earthly power; afterwards, each thought the other better than himself and sought to excel in humble ministry to the saints. Peter charged home the crowd with the murder of the Son of God, until the rabble became a congregation and thousands cried for mercy. Can you recognize in him the timid son of Jonas who dared not face the question of a servant girl? And what made the difference? From the first, they had enjoyed the teaching and grace of the Holy Spirit. Though not given in fullness (John 7:39), yet He was working on human hearts (Luke 2:25–27). Indeed, our Lord had breathed on them and said, "Receive ye the Holy Ghost" (John 20:22) before He went on to say, "Ye shall be baptized with the Holy Ghost not many days hence" (Acts 1:5). What does this mean, except that those who have already received the Spirit in a lower measure may look for and receive His gracious filling—grace on grace, wave on wave, flood on flood?

The same truth is taught by contrast between Romans 7, an arid wilderness marked by one or two green spots, and Romans 8, a very garden of the Lord full of murmuring streams from Lebanon, bringing fertility and beauty into all lives where they come. One chapter describes a life that lacks the fullness of the Spirit, while the other rings from end to end with mention of His person, offices, and work.

Can you not see here the reason for the failure and disappointment of your life? You are living experimentally on the other side of Pentecost. The Holy Spirit is in you, but He does not fill you. You are trying to live a Christian life in the neglect of the one power by which this marvel can be achieved. What wonder that you fail and are often inclined to give up in despair because your ideal is so far beyond your reach. What wonder that your closest friends sadly contrast the luxuriance of your promises with the meagerness of your fruit. It is hardly necessary to ask if you received the filling of the Holy Spirit when you believed. It is but too patent that you did not; and if in this hour of unusual thoughtfulness you were led to see your position and seek that holy filling that you may have, there is not the least doubt that you would suddenly rise up into an excellency of Christian living that would be as great a contrast to your past as sunlight to moonlight, and as the profusion of an autumn orchard to the bare and storm-swept trees of winter.

This is the glorious meaning of the Day of Pentecost; it has put within the reach of all—of old men and children, of young men and maidens—that blessed filling of the Spirit, which in former times was reserved for only a few of the most illustrious saints (Acts 2:17–18).

THE BLESSINGS OF THE FILLING

Note the several ways in which this filling of the Spirit would operate.

1. *You would get a new and vivid conception of the Lord Jesus.* Is it not your chief complaint that His figure is so indistinct, and that you are so unable to realize His presence? Are you not disturbed to know that the glimpses of His face are few and far between, and your moments of true communion fitful? The reason is to be found in the feebleness of the Spirit's action in your life. It is His special function to take of the things of Christ and reveal them to us; and one chief symptom of His having filled the soul is that the soul luxuriates in a vivid and abiding recognition of the Lord's real and glorious presence. No, more, Christ dwells in us by the Holy Spirit like the sun dwells in the world as the atmosphere is warmed by its beams (Eph. 3:17).

2. *You would obtain more constant victory over sin.* How many Christians complain of the uprisings of

their old and depraved nature, which so rapidly responds to the suggestions of the tempter, betraying the continued presence in the heart of that self-principle that has been the cause of all the evil and misery of the world! To cope with this is the enigma of many hearts ambitious of saintliness. And of how many is it the bitter regret that length of years and experience and incessant struggles fail to give them victory! This also is largely because there has been no deep experience of the filling of the Holy Spirit.

It is His special work to deal with these uprisings. Without Him the carnal impulses of the self laugh us to scorn, as the tumultuous waves the injunction of Canute. But let Him occupy the heart in His divine glory, and He "lusts against the flesh" so that we may not do the things we would (Gal. 5:17). The law of the Spirit of life in Christ Jesus makes us free from the law of sin and death that is in our members (Rom. 8:2). There is no greater safeguard against impurity and sin than to reckon that the whole personal nature has now become the temple of the Holy Spirit, and to trust Him to keep His own property absolutely for Himself (1 Cor. 6:19).

3. *You would have a more unbroken assurance of acceptance and adoption into the family of God.* To ignore or lessen the work of the Spirit in the heart is to silence the one voice that witnesses with our spirits that we are born of God (Rom. 8:15). What else could the apostle Paul mean when he says, "After that ye believed, ye were sealed with that Holy Spirit of promise, which is the earnest of our inheritance . . ." (Eph. 1:13–14)? Those words surely teach us that what the earnest penny is to the farm laborer, what the first sod is to the purchaser of Scotch estates, what the grapes of Eschol

are to the vintage of Palestine—that is, the guarantee and sample of what has been obtained—the presence of the Holy Spirit in the believer's heart is of the glorious inheritance reserved for us in heaven. It stands to reason, therefore, that the strength and clearness of the Holy Spirit's witness will be in proportion to the fullness of His indwelling. Let us do everything to increase and accentuate the power of this precious testimony to our childship.

4. *You would obtain new power for service.* It is said that when the apostles had prayed, the place where they met was shaken, "and they were all filled with the Holy Ghost, and they spake the Word of God with boldness. . . . And with great power gave the apostles witness of the resurrection of the Lord Jesus" (Acts 4:31, 33). Little enough power may have rested upon your work for God. You have waved the censer between the living and the dead, and the plague has not stayed. You may have spoken the old words that once acted as a charm, but no miracle of grace has followed. You may have plied the weary routine of work from year to year, without winning a single soul for the Master. Oh, what a terrible waste of energy! It is much as if a man were to try to turn a ponderous machine by hand instead of attaching it to the flywheel of a vast engine revolving rapidly but uselessly within his reach.

The Holy Spirit is a Spirit of power, the dynamics of the kingdom of heaven, the energy of the life of God, which can alone vivify dead spirits. The more we have of this, the more certain we are of great spiritual results; while without this, we may sow much but our seed will be lost, and the scanty ears of autumn fail to reward our toils. The life-giving Spirit must be with us in power, or we will never see dead souls awake to the life of God under our word.

5. *You would be kept in mind of your true attitude in Jesus.* We forget so soon. At the onset of evil we do not recollect to look away to Him. Long periods of time pass during which we are but faintly conscious that we are God's adopted children, sharing the victory of our risen Lord and destined to stand forever in the inner circle of God's throne. And this is because the Holy Spirit has so little power in our lives; whereas if only we were filled with Him, He would be in us the Spirit of remembrance, bringing all things to our memory and keeping us in the true posture of all holy souls (John 14:26).

I am not anxious here to distinguish between the filling of the Holy Spirit and the baptism of the Holy Spirit. So far as I can understand it, they are synonymous. In Acts 1:5 our Lord said, "Ye shall be baptized with the Holy Ghost not many days hence." And in Acts 2:4 we are told, "They were all filled with the Holy Ghost." So far as I can understand, therefore, they are one and the same thing, and the writer of the Book of Acts prefers the word *filling*. It recurs like the chime of a peal of bells, borne by the fitful breeze across the valley of the centuries. In any case, let us see to it that we know what the filling is; it will be time enough then to discuss the baptism.

THE APPROPRIATION OF
THE FILLING

Say not that this filling by the Spirit was for the first Christians and not for us. Certainly His gifts were part of the special endowments needed to impress the Gentile world; but the filling of the Spirit is conterminous with no one age. Alas, many think that the Almighty, like some bankrupt builder, constructed the portico of His church with marble and has finished it with common brick! But what does the apostle mean (Eph. 5:18) when he bids us, "Be filled with the Spirit"? We appropriate the doctrines, the exhortations, and the mystic teachings of that glorious epistle; why then should we overlook this distinct command, which demands the obedience of all to whom the epistle comes? Let us never forget also that God's biddings are His enablings, and that what He commands the universal church He is prepared to accomplish for each individual member of it.

Nothing could be clearer than the announcement of the apostle Peter on the Day of Pentecost, that the promise of the Spirit was not to themselves only but "to all that are afar off, even as many as the Lord our God shall call" (Acts 2:39). Have you been called to the grace of God? Then the promise of being filled is as much for you in the westering light of this age as it was for those who lived in its silver dawn. Appropriate it.

1. *You must appropriate the filling power of the Holy Spirit as we do all of God's gifts—by faith.* Do not prepare yourself to receive it. Do not attempt a renovation of your inner life as the condition for His entrance, for your utmost preparations will be made in vain. Do not try to make room for Him. Simply be willing to yield your whole being to His grace and believe that, just as the earthly parent gives to the child all good and needful things as soon as the request is made, so will our Father in heaven give the filling of His Spirit to each child who asks for it. Ask for it in humble consciousness of your own unworthiness but with eager desire that you may be better able to glorify God. Wait in the surrender and stillness of your heart, like that which hushed the tabernacle before the ark where Samuel slept. Believe that there and then God does keep

His word with your soul, and that "the LORD, whom ye seek, shall suddenly come to his temple" (Mal. 3:1).

Then rise up and go forth from your chamber, not trying to feel filled, but reckoning that God has kept His word with you; dare·to believe it, though you may not be conscious of any emotional outburst. And you will find when you come to work or suffer or meet temptation, that there will be in you the consciousness of a power that you have never known before, which will indicate the filling of the Holy Spirit.

2. *But remember it is not enough to be filled once for all.* Like the apostles of old, we must seek perpetual refillings. They who were filled in the second chapter of Acts were filled again in the fourth. Happy is that man who never leaves his chamber in the morning without definitely seeking and receiving the plenitude of the Spirit! He will be a proficient scholar in God's school, for the new anointing, which he has received like fresh oil, will abide in him and teach him all things. Above all, he will be taught the secret of abiding fellowship with Christ, for it is written, "As it hath taught you, ye shall abide in him" (1 John 2:27).

3. *It is all-important also to remember that just as a fire cannot be maintained without freshly heaped-up fuel, so the energetic working of the Holy Spirit in human hearts is largely dependent on the daily devout study of the Word of God.* It is through the Word that the Spirit effects the fullness of His work on those that receive Him.

There is nothing more to be said now. It is doubtless true that we may be filled with the Holy Spirit from our conversion; but since this is not the general experience of Christians, let us examine where we stand. And if needs be, let us ask for that which might have been ours long years ago, if only we had sought it.

THE SECRET
OF POWER

THE SECRET
OF POWER

O you not sometimes moan over your want of power? You stand face to face with devil-tormented people, but you cannot cast the devil out. You feel that you ought to confess Christ in the workshop, the commercial room, the railway carriage, and the home, but your lips refuse to utter the message of the heart. Yes, and worse than all, you are constantly being overcome by besetting sins, which carry you whither you would not. There is a lamentable lack of power among us. Not many can roll back the tide of battle from the gates, nor wield the weapons, which were child's play to the saints of olden times.

I learned a lesson about this the other day in my firewood factory, where we provide employment for men and boys. We use a circular saw for cutting through the beams of solid timber. Until recently, this saw was worked by a crank, turned by twelve to fifteen men. But it was slow, hard, and expensive work. At last we were driven to something more expeditious and bought a gas engine. Now the saw, driven by this engine, does in two or three hours as much work as it did formerly in a day, and at less than a tenth of the cost. It is the same saw, but the difference lies in the power that drives it. It used to be driven by hand power; now it is driven by an equivalent for steam, and the only thing we need to do is to keep the connecting band tight.

It is not a question of our abilities or qualifications, but of the power behind us. If that is nothing more than human, it is not surprising that the results of our efforts are miserably poor. But if we link ourselves to the eternal power of God, nothing will be impossible to us. "All things are possible to him that believeth" (Mark 9:23). The greater matter is to see that the connecting band of our faith is in good use.

"But where can I find the power of God?" you may wonder.

Jesus Christ is the reservoir in which the power of God is stored. "It pleased the Father that in him should all fulness dwell" (Col. 1:19). All power is His. He would not receive it from the Devil on the mountain of temptation, but He laid claim to it on the mountain of ascension. Listen to His majestic words, "All power is given unto me in heaven and in earth" (Matt. 28:18). In that august moment He united in Himself the power that He had as the Son of Man with the power He had with the Father before the world was. And now all power resides in Him forevermore, not for Himself only, but for us.

"How may I get this power for myself?" you ask.

By faith. Each time you are face-to-face with some difficulty or temptation or call to service, lift up your heart to the living Savior, draw upon Him, let Him know that you are depending upon Him for the word to say and the strength to say it. Immediately there will be a welling up of power within your heart, as lakes are filled from hidden springs.

"But my faith is so weak that I forget to look in my hour of need," you protest. "And when I do look, it does not seem to give me much help."

Weak faith generally shows that there is something wrong in the inner life. Examine yourselves to see the cause. Are you yielding to temptation? Every temptation overcome is an increase of spiritual power, but every temptation yielded to cuts the sinews of your strength and shears off the seven locks of your might. Have you fully yielded yourself to God? Often failure points to lack of consecration. Is not self too prominent in you? Before conversion you lived from the center of an irreligious self. Are you perfectly sure that you are not now living from the center of a religious self?

"Show me the workings of this religious self, the symptom and source of weakness," you say, "that I may know and hate myself."

Think for a moment! In making plans for doing God's work, do you not often act upon your own impulse instead of waiting to inquire His will? Have you not often rushed into an enterprise without considering whose spirit it was that prompted you? Do you not continually ask God to help you in all your little schemes, without first asking if He approved of them or seeking to know what He had on hand, and if you might help Him? And when all is done, is there not a spirit of self-congratulation, which, though it array itself in the garb of humility, is most distasteful to Him who "resisteth the proud" (James 4:6)?

"How may I be different? I am prepared to forego anything, if only I may win this secret of blessing and saving others."

Then yield to Jesus your whole self. You are His by the purchase of His blood; now be His by your own glad choice. Bind yourself as a sacrifice to the horns of the altar. Present your body, soul, and spirit. Hand yourself over to be His. Ask Him to come and take you. Tell Him that, from this glad hour, you wish to be made willing to have His way, His will, His law in all. Go through life saying a thousand times each day, "I am His!"

Your mind still is not settled: "But if I try to give myself thus wholly to Him, how will I know that He takes me?"

At the first, you can only know it by faith. He pledges His word to take that which is given Him (John 6:37). If you give yourself, or try to give yourself, or will to give yourself, He instantly takes you to be His; and from that moment you are His in the bonds of an ownership that is the daybreak of God's love and power and blessing. At first there may be no gracious response of emotion; but as the days pass on and you come to taste more and more the sweetness of belonging, nevermore to yourself but only to Him, there will come into your heart the fullness of joy as well as the fullness of power. You may not be conscious of having much power, or any, before you begin to work in the Spirit; but when you have begun you will be aware that there is going forth from you a virtue that will make the commonest words as powerful as that garment hem that brought healing to the trembling woman.

"But how will I remain in this blessed state?"

Jesus will see to that. Trust Him to keep you

trusting. At first it may be an effort to keep yourself in the love of God, but it will become easier until at last it is a second nature. Then you will think more of what He says to you than of what you say to Him. Then you will be always on the alert to catch the least whisper of His voice, the slightest token of His will. Then you will bring every plan and purpose into the King's weighing house before putting them in action or even submitting them to your dearest friend. Then you will always feel that you are a member of His body, depending for the least direction and for all needed strength on Him, the Head. Then there will be ever on your lips the words, "What next, dear Lord, what next?" And you will read His will in circumstances that to others might seem trivial and devoid of meaning. You will be always on the alert to find out for each day what good works have been prepared by Him for you. All that happens to you will be as couriers bringing the secret letters of His love, signed by His hand and telling you what to do. Nothing will seem to come amiss or by chance. In all things you will have definite fellowship with Him until you talk over with Him all your life. You will abide in Him, and He in you, and out of that abiding union will come abiding power, because His power will reside in you in all its glory, just as the flashing volume of the cataract dwells constantly in the rocky basin into which it falls, from which it rushes forth to quench drought and famine from the fields and homes of men.

"It is a fair vision, and I would that my poor life might touch even its outermost rim of beauty, but I fear it is not for me."

But it is, if only you are content to open the door to Him. He stands at the door and knocks; if any will open the door He will come in (Rev. 3:20). Are you willing to let Him in? Are you willing for him to do what He likes with you and yours? Are you willing to be an ass's jawbone in the hands of this Samson, or a cipher behind that mighty numeral? If so, Christ will begin to fulfill in you the pleasure of His goodness and the work of faith with power; and you may write on the lintel of your life, "This house has passed into other hands and will be opened under entirely new management." You cannot help being full of power if the Almighty Savior comes to live in you. If you want overcoming power, get the Overcomer to come and fill you, and the thing is done. Do not talk about *it,* but about Him; it is not an influence, it is Christ Himself.

This is my will, most merciful Lord, and from this moment grant that I may always desire and will that which is to You most acceptable and most dear. Let Your will be mine. Let my will ever follow Yours and agree perfectly with it, as the steel to the magnet or the handle to the head.

But there is something in addition that you must mark and remember. The reading of the Bible is as necessary as the fueling of an engine with coal, or the imparting of strength to an invalid by food. And this reading must be steeped in the spirit of prayer. You must never let your work for Christ so engross you as to rob you of those quiet hours when He calls you to be alone with Him, that He may declare to you His Father's name, reveal Himself, and charge you with the spiritual forces stored up within Him. It will be well to keep yourself free from attractive avenues of service to be fresh for those still hours. They are more dear to Him and more needful for you than all your service.

"In earing time and in harvest thou shalt rest" (Exod. 34:21). One hour spent in work, after prolonged fellowship with Christ, will pay better than twelve hours spent in unbroken toils. Christ cares less for the amount of work done than for its quality. He is more anxious about the worker than the work.

Help me to remember this, O Lord of the harvest. And often may I leave even the whitening fields, that in You I may find rest and strength. And if I seem to tarry, I pray, send some loving reminder to call me to Your side, as You called to Mary by the hand of her sister Martha.

Stay one moment. There is one blessed secret more. When the apostles were eager to win the world, Christ kept them waiting for ten long days, not because He was indifferent to the claims of a perishing race, nor to dampen their ardor, but because they had not received that enduement of power that is the prerogative of the Holy Spirit to impart. Perhaps you lack this. You have received the Holy Spirit as comforter, teacher, sanctifier, but not yet as power for service. But He will be this to you, if you will allow Him. "Be filled with the Spirit" is a positive command. All you have to do is to make room for Him, and this sacred wind will come in through every chink and keyhole and aperture of your life; you will unconsciously become filled with spiritual might, "strengthened with might by his Spirit in the inner man" (Eph. 3:16). And when the power of the Almighty overshadows our meek and waiting souls, who can estimate the results that shall accrue to His glory? This is the crying need of the church. This is the one condition of her success. But it can only be hers by prayer and fasting. If only she would never rest till she obtained it—watching daily at His gates, waiting at the posts of His doors, seeking it as silver, and searching for it as a hidden treasure—then she would do exploits as of old and look forth as the morning, "fair as the moon, clear as the sun, and terrible as an army with banners" (Song of Sol. 6:10).

If you win this power, beware that you do not lose it. If a man sits on a chair, the feet of which stand on glass casters, and you pour a continual stream of electricity into him, not a spark will be lost; every part of his body will be charged with it. But if there is so much as a thread connecting his body with the earth, all the electric current will pass away, as water through the cracks of a jar. So will one besetting sin, one evil motive, one proud thought indulged in and permitted, rob us of the might of the Holy Spirit. Let us beware!

"And the LORD looked upon him, and said, Go in this thy might . . . : have not I sent thee?" (Judg. 6:14).

THE LOST CHORD
FOUND

THE LOST CHORD
FOUND

HE story of the lost chord has been told in exquisite verse and in stately music. We have all heard of the lady who, in the autumn twilight that softly filled the room, laid her fingers on the open keys of a glorious organ. She knew not what she was playing or what she was dreaming then; but she struck one chord of music, like the sound of a great amen.

> *It flooded the crimson twilight,*
> *   Like the close of an angel's psalm,*
> *And it lay on my fevered spirit*
> *   With a touch of infinite calm.*
>
> *It quieted pain and sorrow,*
> *   Like love overcoming strife;*
> *It seemed the harmonious echo*
> *   From our discordant life.*

> *It linked all perplexed meanings*
> *Into one perfect peace,*
> *And trembled away into silence,*
> *As if it were loth to cease.*
> *—Adelaide Anne Procter*

Something called her away, and when she returned to the organ she had lost that chord divine. Though she longed for it and sought it, all was in vain. It was a lost chord.

OUR SAD EXPERIENCE

Whenever I hear that story, it reminds me of the lost joy, the lost peace, the lost power of which so many complain. It seems as if they had struck the chord of a blessed and glorious life at the beginning of their Christian experience. As long as those notes lingered in their lives, they were like days of heaven upon earth. But alas! They died away soon into silence—and all life is now filled with longing for the grace of days that are dead.

> *Where is the blessedness I knew*
> *When first I saw the Lord?*
> *Where is the soul-refreshing view*
> *Of Jesus and Wis Word?*
>
> *What peaceful hours I then enjoyed!*
> *How sweet their memory still!*
> *But they have left an aching void,*
> *The world can never fill.*

These words are written to help all who feel such remorse, to give them again the sweet lost chord. Take heart! You may again have all, and more than all, that you have ever lost. You have flung your precious stones into the deep; there has been a moment's splash, a tiny ripple, and they have sunk down and down, apparently beyond hope of recovery. Yet the hand of Christ will again place them on your palm. Only henceforth be wise enough to let him keep them for you.

THE WAY BACK

These are the steps back, steps you may take at once:

1. *Be sure that God will give you a hearty welcome.* God is not an angry judge. He has not given you up or ceased to love you. He longs after you. His portrait is drawn by one who could not mislead us, who compares Him to the father of a loved and prodigal boy, ever watching from his windows the road by which the truant went, eagerly longing for his return and ready, if he should see him a great way off, to run to meet him and clasp him, rags and filth and all, to his yearning heart. That is your God, my friend. Listen to His words, broken by sighs: "How shall I give thee up, Ephraim? how shall I deliver thee, Israel? how shall I make thee as Admah? how shall I set thee as Zeboim? mine heart is turned within me, my repentings are kindled together" (Hos. 11:8). Read the last chapter of the Book of Hosea, which may be well called the backsliders' gospel. Read the third chapter of Jeremiah, and let the plaintive pleadings to return soak into your spirit. Read the story of Peter's fall and restoration, and let your tears fall thick and fast on John 21, as you learn how delicately the Lord forgave and how generously

He entrusted the backslider with His sheep and His lambs. Be sure that though your repeated failures and sins have worn out everyone else, they have not exhausted the infinite love of God. He tells us to forgive our offending brother unto 490 times; how much more often will He forgive us? As the height of heaven above the earth, so great is His mercy. "Let the wicked forsake his way, and the unrighteous man his thoughts: and let him return unto the LORD, and he will have mercy upon him: and to our God, for he will abundantly pardon" (Isa. 55:7). If you go back to God, you are sure of a hearty welcome.

2. *Seek to know and confess whatever has come between God and you.* You have lost the light of God's face, not because He has arbitrarily withdrawn it, but because your iniquities have come between you and your God. Your sins, like a cloud before the sun, have hid His face from you. Do not spend time looking at them as a whole; deal with them one by one. The Boer is a formidable foe to British soldiers because he is trained from boyhood to take a definite aim and bring down his mark, while our soldiers fire in volleys. In dealing with sin, we should imitate the Boer soldier in the definiteness and accuracy of his aim. Ask God to search you and show you what wicked way is in you. Marshal all your life before Him, as Joshua marshaled Israel; sift it through, tribe by tribe, family by family, household by household, man by man, until at last you find the Achan who has robbed you of the blessed smile of God. Do not say, "Lord, I am a great sinner, I have done what I ought not, I have not done what I ought." But say, "Lord, I have sinned in this, and this, and that, and the other." Call up each rebel sin, by its right name, to receive sentence of death. Your heart is choked with

90

sins; empty it out, as you would empty a box, by handing out first the articles that lie on the surface. When you have removed them, you will see more underneath; hand them out also. When these are removed, you will probably see some more. Never rest till all are gone. Confession is this process of telling God the unvarnished story—the sad, sad story—of each accursed sin, how it began, how you sinfully permitted it to grow, how you have loved and followed it to your bitter cost.

3. *Believe in God's instant forgiveness.* How long does it take you to forgive your child, when you are sure that child is really sorry and repentant? Time is not considered in the forgiveness. The estrangement of a lifetime and the wrongdoing of years may be forgiven in the twinkling of an eye, in the time that a tear takes to form and fall. So is it with God. If we confess our sins, He is faithful and just to forgive us (1 John 1:9). He does sometimes keep us waiting for an answer to other prayers; but He never keeps us waiting a single second for an answer to our prayer for forgiveness. It is hardly possible for the prodigal to stammer out the words, "Father, I have sinned," before the answer flashes upon him: "I have put away your sin; you shall not die." There is not a moment's interval between the humble and sad telling of the story of sin and God's forgiveness. As soon as a penitent appears in the doorway of God's throne room, the golden scepter of His royal forgiveness is stretched out for that person to touch. You may not feel forgiven. You may have no ecstasy of joy. But you are forgiven in the thoughts of God. The angels hear Him say, "Child, your sins are all forgiven thee. Go in peace." If we confess, and as soon as we confess, He is faithful and just to forgive. He

never says, "Go your way and return tomorrow, and I will see whether I can forgive." He hates the sin and is only too glad to sweep it away. He loves the sinner and is only too happy to receive him again to His embrace. God is able to do all this so quickly and so entirely because Jesus Christ our Lord "bare our sins in his own body on the tree" (1 Peter 2:24).

4. *Give up the cause of past failure.* True repentance shows itself in eager care not to offend again. This care prompts the sinner to go back on his past life to discover how it was that he came to sin, and to avoid the cause. Is it a friendship? Then he will cut the tender cord, though it were the thread of his life. Is it an amusement? Then he will forever absent himself from that place, those scenes, and that companionship. Is it a profitable means of making money? Then he will rather live on a crust than follow it a moment longer. Is it a study, a pursuit, a book? Then he will rather lose hand, or foot, or eye, than miss the favor of God, which is life. Is it something that the church permits? Nevertheless to him it will be sin. If you cannot walk on ice without slipping or falling, it is better not to go on at all. If you cannot digest certain food, it is better not to put it in the mouth. It may seem impossible to extricate yourself from certain entanglements that have woven themselves about you; nevertheless remember Him who said, "Let my people go, that they may serve me" (Exod. 8:1). He cut the knot for them; if you trust Him, He will cut it for you. Or if He does not cut it at a single blow, He will untie it by the patient workings of His providence.

5. *Take any public step that may be necessary.* It is not enough to confess to God; you must also confess to man, supposing that you have sinned against him.

"Leave there thy gift before the altar, and go thy way; first be reconciled to thy brother . . ." (Matt. 5:24). If you have done him a wrong, go and tell him so. If you have defrauded him, whether he knows or not, send him the amount you have taken or kept back and add to it something to compensate him for his loss. Under the Levitical law the delinquent restored that which he took violently away or that about which he had dealt falsely, and added one-fifth part thereto; only then might one come with a trespass offering to the priest and be forgiven. I believe this principle holds good today. You never will be happy till you have made restitution. Write the letter or make the call at once. And if the one whom you defrauded is no longer alive, then make the debt right with his heirs and representatives. You must roll away this stone from the grave or the dead joy can never arise, however loudly you may call it to come forth. I do not believe in a repentance that is not noble enough to make amends for the past, so far as they may lie within reach.

6. *Give your whole heart once and forever to God.* You may have done it before; but do it again. You may never have done it; then do it for the first time. Kneel down and give yourself, your life, your interests, your all to God. Lay the sacrifice on the altar. If you cannot *give,* then ask God to come and *take.* Tell Him that you wish to be only, always, all for Him. You might well hesitate to give the glorious Lord such a handful of withered leaves, if He had not expressly asked you to give him your heart. It is very wonderful; but He would not make such a request if He did not really mean it. No doubt He can make something out of your poor nature: a vessel for His use, a weapon for His hand, a receptacle for His glory, a crown for His brow.

7. *Trust God to keep you in all the future.* The old version used to tell us that He was able to keep us from "falling" (Jude 24). The new version, giving a closer rendering of the Greek, tells us that He is able to guard us from "stumbling" (RV). So He can. So He will. But we must trust Him. Moment by moment, we must look into His face and say, "Hold me up, Lord, and I shall be safe. Keep me as the apple of Your eye. Hide me under the shadow of Your wings." He will never fail you. "He will not fail thee, nor forsake thee" (Deut. 31:6). "For he shall give his angels charge over thee, to keep thee in all thy ways" (Ps. 91:11). "He shall cover thee with his feathers, and under his wings shalt thou trust . . ." (v. 4).

But you say, "I fail to look to the Lord at the moment of temptation." Then do this. Ask the Holy Spirit, whose office it is to bring all things to our remembrance (John 14:26), that he would remind you to look to Jesus when you are in danger. Entrust yourself each morning into His hands. Look to Him to keep you looking. Trust in Him to keep you trusting. Do not look at your difficulties or weaknesses. Do not keep thinking that you will someday fall again. Go through life whispering, saying, singing a thousand times a day, "Jesus saves me now."

FREEDOM FROM BACKSLIDING

A friend once told me that she had been kept from backsliding thus: She always took time at night to consider quietly in the presence of God where she had lost ground during the day; and if she felt that she had done so, she never slept until she had asked to be forgiven and restored. It is a good expedient, dear reader, for you and me. Let us repair the little rift within the lute, lest by and by it spread and make our music mute, and slowly widening, silence all.

If these directions are followed, the lost chord will be no longer lost, nor will we have to wait until God's great Angel sounds it, but it will ring again in our hearts and make sweet music in our lives.

Not only so, but as that chord sounds again in our hearts, it will attune our lives to accord with these sublime, heavenly notes that are ever vibrating and thrilling around us. We will translate it into the most common actions of our lives. All things will fall into step with that marching music, and we will know what the apostle meant by saying that our lives may become "God's poem" (Eph. 2:10, lit.).

THE SECRET OF
VICTORY OVER SIN

THE SECRET OF
VICTORY OVER SIN

HE longer I live and learn the experience of other Christian people, the more I long to help them. The more I yearn to unfold glimpses of that life of peace, power, and victory over sin that our heavenly Father has made possible for us. There are blessed secrets in the Bible, hidden from the wise and prudent but revealed to babes, things that eye has not seen, nor ear heard, nor the heart of man conceived. Yet God reveals these secrets by His Spirit to those who love Him; and if these were once understood and accepted, they would wipe away many a tear and shed sunshine on many a darkened pathway.

The most bitter experience with most believers is the presence and power of sin in their lives. They long to walk through this grimy world with pure hearts and stainless garments. But when they would do good, evil is present with them. They consent that God's law is good; they approve it, they delight in it, they endeavor to keep it. Notwithstanding all this, they seem as helpless to perform God's law as a man whose brain has been smitten with paralysis is helpless to walk straight. How many briny tears have fallen upon the open pages of the Penitent's Psalm (Ps. 51), shed by those who could repeat it every word from the heart! And what regiments of weary feet have trodden the Bridge of Sighs, if so we may call Romans 7, which sets forth in vivid force the experience of one who has not learned God's secret!

Surely our God must have provided for all this. It would not have been like Him to fill us with hatred for sin and longings for holiness, if there were no escape from the tyranny of the one and no possibility of attaining the other. It would be a small matter to save us from sinning on the other side of the pearly gate; we want to be saved from sinning now, in this dark world. We want it for the sake of the world, that it may be attracted and convinced of the gospel. We want it for our own peace, which cannot be perfected while we groan under a bondage worse than that of Egypt. We want it for the glory of God, which would then be reflected from our lives with undimming brightness, as sunshine from burnished metal.

THE PROMISES OF GOD

What then does the Word of God lead us to expect? Before Abraham arose to walk through the Land of Promise in its length and breadth, God bade him to "lift up his eyes and look" (Gen. 13:14). And before we can enter the enjoyment of our privileges in Jesus Christ, we must know what they are, in something of the length and breadth and depth and height.

1. *We must not expect to be free from temptation.* Our

adversary the Devil is always going about "as a roaring lion, . . . seeking whom he may devour" (1 Peter 5:8). He tempted our Lord, as he will tempt us. He will entice us to do wrong by every avenue of sense and will pour his evil suggestions through eye, ear, finger, tongue, and mind. If he does not attack us himself, he can set on us any one of his myriad agents, who will get behind us and step softly up to us, whispering grievous blasphemies that we will think have proceeded from our own minds.

But temptation is not sin. A man may ask me to share the spoils of a burglary, but no one can accuse me of receiving stolen property if I indignantly refuse and keep my door shut against him. Our Lord "was in all points tempted like as we are, yet without sin" (Heb. 4:15). A person might go through hell itself, teeming with all manner of awful suggestions, and yet not sin. God would not allow Satan to tempt us if temptation necessarily led to sin; but temptation does not do so. There is no sin so long as the will refuses to consent to the solicitation or snap at the bait.

Temptation may even be a blessing to someone, if it reveals that person's weakness and drives him to the Almighty Savior. Do not be surprised, then, dear child of God, if you are tempted at every step of your earthly journey and almost beyond your endurance. Remember that God "will not suffer you to be tempted above that ye are able; but will with the temptation also make a way to escape, that ye may be able to bear it" (1 Cor. 10:13).

2. *We must not expect to lose our sinful nature.* When we are born again, a new life—the life of God—is put into us by the Holy Spirit. But the old self-life, which is called in Scripture "the flesh," is not taken away. The

two may co-exist in the same heart. "For the flesh lusteth against the Spirit, and the Spirit against the flesh . . ." (Gal. 5:17). The presence of this old self-life within our hearts may be detected by its risings, rufflings, chafings, and movings toward sin when temptation calls to it from without. It may be as still as death before the increasing power of the new life, but it will still be present in the depths of our nature, as a Samson in the dark dungeons of Philistia; and there will always be a possibility, and a fear, of its strength growing again to our shame and hurt.

Do not ignore the presence of a sinful nature within you, with its tendencies and possibilities for sin. Many souls have been betrayed into negligence and unwatchfulness by the idea that the root of sin had been plucked from their hearts, and that therefore they could not sin again. And in the face of some sudden uprising of their old nature, they have been filled with agony and shame, even if they have not dropped for a moment back into the sea of black ink. "If we say that we have no sin, we deceive ourselves, and the truth is not in us" (1 John 1:8).

There is a difference between *sin* and *sins*. *Sin* is the root principle of all evil—the flesh, the old self-life, the bias and tendency to sin, which may be kept down by the grace of God but which will remain in us, though in diminishing power, until we leave this world. *Sins* are the outcome of this, the manifestations in fact of the sinful nature within; from these we may be daily saved through the grace of Jesus (Matt. 1:21). To put the matter clearly, *sin* is not dead in us, but we may be dead to *sin,* so that it will not bear the deadly fruit of *sins.*

3. *We must not expect to be free from liability to sin.* What is sin? It is the yes of the human will to

temptation. It is very difficult to express the delicate workings of our hearts, but does not something like this happen when we are tempted? A temptation is suddenly presented to us and makes a strong appeal. Immediately, there may be a tumultuous movement of the old nature, as the strings of a violin or piano vibrate in answer to any sounds that may be trilling in the air around. Some do not feel this tremulous response of the old nature, while others do; though I believe that it will get fainter and fainter as a person treats it with continued neglect, so that at last in the mature saint it will become almost inaudible. This response indicates the presence of the evil nature within, which is in itself hateful in the sight of our holy God. The evil nature should be confessed and ever needs the presence of the blood of Jesus to counteract and atone for it. But that tremulous movement of the old nature has not as yet developed into an actual overt sin for which we are responsible and of which we need to repent.

Sin is an act of the will and is only possible when the will assents to some unholy influence. The Tempter presents his temptation through the senses and emotions to make an appeal to the will, which is the real self. Suppose that the will instantly shudders, as when chicks shudder to see a hawk hovering in the sky above them. Suppose that the will cries, "How can I do this great wickedness, and sin against God?" Suppose that the will looks at once to Jesus. In such a case, so far as I can understand, there are no sins. If, on the other hand, the will begins to palter with temptation, to dally with it, to consider yielding to it, then we have stepped out of the light and into the darkness. We have broken God's law, splashed our white robes of spiritual purity, and brought ourselves into condemnation. To this tendency we are liable as long as we are in this world. We may live godly, righteous, sober lives for years; but if we look away from God for only a moment, our wills may be suddenly mastered, as Louis XVIII was mastered by the mobs that invaded his palace. We may, like King David, be hurried into a sin that will blast our peace and blacken our character for all time.

THE SECRETS OF VICTORY

Now what are the secrets of victory over sin?

1. *Remember that the blood of Jesus is ever at work cleansing you.* It is sweet to notice the present tenses of Scripture. The Bible says that Jesus forgives, heals, redeems, crowns, satisfies, and executes judgment; but the sweetest statement of all is, "The blood of Jesus Christ . . . cleanseth us from all sin" (1 John 1:7). It cleansed us when we first knelt at His cross. It will cleanse away the last remnant of sin when we cross the golden threshold of eternity. But it also cleanses us every hour, as the brook flows over the stones in its bed till they glisten with lustrous beauty. Our possession of a sinful nature is an evil that ever needs an antidote. The risings and stirrings of that nature beneath the appeals of temptation ever need cleansing. The permission of things in our lives—which we now count harmless, but which we will someday condemn and put away—all these need God's forgiveness. For all these needs there is ample provision in the blood of Jesus, which is always crying to God for us. Even when we do not plead the blood, or remember it, or realize our need of it, it fulfills for us and in us its unceasing ministry of blessing.

2. *Reckon yourself dead to the appeals of sin.* Sin has

no power over a dead man. Dress it in its most bewitching guise, yet it stirs him not. Tears and smiles and words and blows fail to awaken a response from a corpse. No appeal will stir it now, until it hears the voice of the Son of God. This is our position in regard to the appeals of sin. God looks on us as having been crucified with Christ, being dead with Him. In Him we have passed out of the world of sin and death into the world of resurrection glory. This is our position in the mind of God; it is for us to take up this position and make it real by faith. We may not feel any great difference in our status, but we must believe that there is; we must act as if there is. Our children sometimes play make-believe. We too are to make believe we are dead to sin, and we will soon come to feel as we believe. So when a temptation solicits you, say, "I am dead to you. Do not spend your energies on one that is oblivious to your spells and callous to your charms. You have no more power over my Lord and my Head."

"Reckon ye also yourselves to be dead indeed unto sin, but alive unto God through Jesus Christ our Lord" (Rom. 6:11).

3. *Walk in the Spirit; keep in step with the Holy Spirit.* The Holy Spirit is in the heart of every believer (Rom. 8:9); but alas, too often He is shut up in some mere attic in the back of the house while the world fills the rest. And as long as it is so, there is only one long story of defeat and unrest. But the Spirit is not content. "Know ye not that the Spirit, which he hath made to dwell in us, yearneth even unto jealous envy?" (James 4:5 RV). Happy are they who yield to Him. Then He will fill them, as the tide fills the harbor and lifts the barges off the banks of mud. He will dwell in them, shedding

abroad the perfume of the love of Jesus, and He will reveal the deep things of God. We can always tell when we are wrong with the Spirit of God; our conscience darkens in a moment when we have grieved Him. And if we are aware of such a darkness, we do well not to rest until we have discovered the cause, confessed it, and put it away. Besides this, if we live and walk in the Spirit, we will find that He will work against the risings of our old nature, counteracting them as a disinfecting powder counteracts the germs of disease, so that "ye may not do the things that ye would" (Gal. 5:17 RV). This is one of the most precious words of the New Testament. If you have never tried it, I invite you to begin testing it in your daily experience. "Walk by the Spirit" hour by hour, in watchful obedience to His slightest promptings, and you will find that "you will not fulfill the lust of the flesh."

4. *As soon as you are aware of temptation, look instantly to Jesus.* Flee to him quicker than a chick runs beneath the shelter of its mother's wing when the kestrel is in the air. When the Tempter comes, look up instantly and say, "Jesus, I am trusting you to keep me." This is what the apostle Paul calls "taking the shield of faith" (Eph. 6:16). The upward glance of faith puts Jesus as a shield between the Tempter and yourself. You may go through life saying a hundred times a day, "Jesus saves me," for He will never let those who trust in Him be ashamed. "He is able to guard you [even] from stumbling" (Jude 24 RV). You may be pressed by temptations from without and feel the workings of evil from within; yet your will, looking earnestly to Jesus, will remain steadfast, immovable, and unyielding. No weapon that is forged against you in the armory of hell will prosper.

There is something even better than this. It was first taught me by a gray-haired clergyman in the study of his deanery at Southampton. When tempted to feel great irritation, he told us that he looked up and claimed the patience and gentleness of Christ; and since then it had become the practice of his life to claim from Christ any virtue of which he felt a deficiency in himself. In hours of unrest, "Your peace, Lord." In hours of irritation, "Your patience, Lord." In hours of temptation, "Your purity, Lord." In hours of weakness, "Your strength, Lord." This was to me a message straight from the throne of God. Till then I had been content with ridding myself of burdens; now I began to reach forth to positive blessing, making each temptation the occasion for a new acquisition of gold leaf. Try it.

CAUSES OF FAILURE

When I have spoken thus, I have sometimes been met by the objection, "Yes, it is quite true that the Lord will keep me if I look to Him; but I often forget to look to Him *in time.*"

This arises from one of three causes. *Perhaps the heart and life have never been entirely surrendered to Jesus.* Constant defeat indicates that there has been failure in consecration. You must not expect Christ to keep you unless you have given your heart and life entirely over to Him, so that He is King. Christ cannot be Keeper if He is not King. And He will not be King at all unless He is King in all. *Or perhaps there is a want of watchfulness.* Christ will not keep us if we carelessly and wantonly put ourselves into the way of temptation. He will give His angels charge over us in every path of duty, not to catch us every time when we like to throw ourselves from the beetling height. "Watch and pray, that ye enter not into temptation" (Matt. 26:41). *Or perhaps there is a lack of feeding on the Word of God.* No one can live a life of faith without seasons of prolonged waiting on God in the loving study of the Bible and in prayer. The person who does not make time for private devotion in the early morning cannot walk with God all day. And of the two things, the devout meditation on the Word is more important to one's soul health than even prayer. It is more needful for you to hear God's words than that God should hear yours, though one will always lead to the other. Attend to these conditions, and it will become both easy and natural to trust Christ in the hour of trial.

If, notwithstanding all these helps, you should be still betrayed into a sin and overtaken by a fault, do not lose heart. If a sheep and a sow fall into a ditch, the sow wallows in it while the sheep bleats piteously until she is cleansed. Likewise the sincere Christian knows when he has sinned. Go at once to your compassionate Savior. Tell Him in the simplest words the story of your fall and sorrow. Ask Him to wash you at once and restore your soul and, while you are asking, believe that it is done. Then go to anyone against whom or with whom you may have sinned; "confess your faults to one another" (James 5:16). Thus, the peace of God that passes all understanding will return to your heart, to guard it like a sentry angel in shining armor.

And if you thus live, free from the power of sin, you will find that the Master will begin to use you as never before and tell you His heart secrets, opening to you the royal magnificence of a life hidden with Himself in God.

HOW TO BEAR
SORROW

HOW TO BEAR
SORROW

OU are passing through a time of deep sorrow. The love on which you were trusting has suddenly failed you and dried up like a brook in the desert—now a dwindling stream, then shallow pools, and at last drought. You are always listening for footsteps that do not come, waiting for a word that is not spoken, pining for a reply that tarries overdue.

Perhaps the savings of your life have suddenly disappeared. Instead of helping others, you must be helped. Or you must leave the warm nest where you have been sheltered from life's storms to go alone into an unfriendly world. Or you are suddenly called to assume the burden of some other life, taking no rest for yourself till you have steered it through dark and difficult seas into the haven. Your health, or sight, or nervous energy is failing. You carry in yourself the sentence of death, and the anguish of anticipating the future is almost unbearable. Perhaps there is the sense of recent loss through death, like the gap in the forest glade where the woodsman has lately been felling trees.

At such times life seems almost insupportable. Will every day be as long as this? Will the slow moving hours ever again quicken their pace? Will life ever array itself in another garb than the torn autumn remnants of past summer glory? Has God forgotten to be gracious? Has He in anger shut up His tender mercies? Is His mercy gone forever?

A UNIVERSAL EXPERIENCE

This road has been trodden by myriads. When you think of the desolating wars that have swept through every century and devastated every land; of the expeditions of the Nimrods, the Nebuchadnezzars, the Napoleons of history; of the merciless slave trade that has never ceased to decimate Africa; and of all the tyranny, the oppression, the wrong that the weak and defenseless have suffered at the hands of their fellows; of the unutterable sorrows of women and children—surely you must see that by far the larger number of our race have passed through the same bitter griefs as those that rend your heart. Jesus Christ himself trod this difficult path, leaving traces of His blood on its flints; and apostles, prophets, confessors, and martyrs have passed by the same way. It is comforting to know that others have traversed the same dark valley and that the great multitudes that stand before the Lamb, waving palms of victory, came out of great tribulation. Where they were, we are; and by God's grace, where they are we shall be.

Yet what steps should we take to deal with the experience of sorrow?

WHAT TO DO IN SORROW

1. *Do not talk about God's punishment.* You may talk of chastisement or correction, for our Father deals with us as with sons; or you may speak of reaping the results of mistakes and sins dropped as seeds into life's furrows in former years; or you may have to bear the consequences of the sins and mistakes of others. But do not speak of your trial as punishment. Surely all the guilt and penalty of sin were laid on Jesus, and He put them away forever. His were the stripes and the chastisement of our peace. If God punishes us for our sins, it would seem that the sufferings of Christ were incomplete; and if He once began to punish us, life would be too short for the infliction of all that we deserve. Besides, how could we explain the anomalies of life and the heavy sufferings of the saints, compared with the gay life of the ungodly? Surely, if our sufferings were penal, there would be a reversal of these lots.

2. *Remember that sorrow is a refiner's crucible.* It may be caused by the neglect or cruelty of another, by circumstances over which the sufferer has no control, or as the direct result of some dark hour in the long past. But inasmuch as God has permitted it to come, it must be accepted as His appointment and considered as the furnace by which He is searching, testing, probing, and purifying the soul. Suffering searches us as fire does metals. We think we are fully for God until we are exposed to the cleansing fire of pain; then we discover, as Job did, how much dross there is in us and how little real patience, resignation, and faith. Nothing so detaches us from the things of this world, the life of sense, and the birdlime of earthly affections. There is probably no other way by which the power of the self-life can be

arrested, so that the life of Jesus may be manifested in our mortal flesh.

But God always keeps the discipline of sorrow in His own hands. Our Lord said, "My Father is the husbandman" (John 15:1). His hand holds the pruning knife. His eye watches the crucible. His gentle touch is on the pulse while the operation is in progress. He will not allow even the Devil to have his own way with us. As in the case of Job, so always. The moments are carefully allotted. The severity of the test is exactly determined by the reserves of grace and strength that are lying unrecognized within us but will be sought and used beneath the severe pressure of pain. He holds the winds in His fist and the waters in the hollow of His hand. He dare not risk the loss of that which has cost Him the blood of His Son. "God is faithful, who will not suffer you to be *tried* above that ye are able" (1 Cor. 10:13, lit.).

3. *Remember that in sorrow the Comforter is near.* God is "very present . . . in time of trouble" (Ps. 46:1). He *sits* by the crucible as a refiner of silver, regulating the heat, marking every change, waiting patiently for the scum to float away so that His own face is mirrored in clear, translucent metal. No earthly friend may tread the winepress with you; but the Savior is there, His garments stained with the blood of the grapes of your sorrow. Dare to repeat it often, though you do not feel it and though Satan insists that God has left you: "Thou art with me" (Ps. 23:4). Mention His name again and again. "*Jesus,* Thou art with me." So you will become conscious that He is there.

When friends come to console you, they talk of time's healing touch, as though the best balm for sorrow were to forget. Or in their well-meant kindness they suggest travel, diversion, amusement, and show their inability to appreciate the black night that hangs over your soul. So you turn from them, sick at heart and prepared to say, as Job of his, "Miserable comforters are ye all" (Job 16:2). But Jesus is nearer than they are, understanding how they wear you, knowing each throb of pain, touched by fellow feeling, silent in a love too full to speak, waiting to comfort from hour to hour as a mother soothes her weary, suffering babe.

Be sure to study the art of this divine comfort, that you may be able to comfort them that are in any affliction with the comfort with which you yourself have been comforted of God (2 Cor. 1:4). There can be no doubt that some trials are permitted to come to us, as to our Lord, for no other reason than that by means of them we should become able to give sympathy and succour to others. And we should watch with all care each symptom of the pain and each prescription of the Great Physician since, in all probability, at some future time we will be called to minister to those passing through similar experiences. Thus, we learn by the things that we suffer and, being made perfect, become authors of priceless and eternal help to souls in agony.

4. *Do not shut yourself up with your sorrow.* A friend in the first anguish of bereavement wrote to me, saying that he must give up the Christian ministries in which he had delighted. I replied immediately, urging him not to do so, because there is no solace for heart pain like ministry. The temptation of great suffering is toward isolation, withdrawal from the life of men, sitting alone, and keeping silence. Do not yield to it. Break through the icy chains of reserve if they have already gathered. Arise, anoint your head, and wash your face; go forth to do your duty, with willing, though

115

chastened, steps. Selfishness of every kind, in its activities or its introspection, is a hurtful thing and shuts out the help and love of God. Sorrow is apt to be selfish. The soul occupied with its own griefs, and refusing to be comforted, becomes presently a Dead Sea, full of brine and salt, over which birds do not fly and beside which no green thing grows. And thus we miss the very lesson that God would teach us. His constant war is against the self-life, and every pain He inflicts is to lessen its hold on us. But we may thwart His purpose and extract poison from His gifts, as men get opium and alcohol from innocent plants.

A beautiful Eastern legend tells us about a Hindu woman who lost her only child. Wild with grief, she implored a prophet to give back her little one to her love. He looked at her for a long while tenderly, and said, "Go, my daughter, bring me a handful of rice from a house into which death has never entered, and I will do as thou desirest." The woman at once began her search. She went from dwelling to dwelling and had no difficulty in locating what the prophet specified; but when the family had granted it, she inquired, "Are you all here around the hearth—father, mother, children—none missing?" But the people invariably shook their heads with sighs and looks of sadness; for far and wide as she wandered, there was always some vacant seat by the hearth. And gradually, as she passed on, the waves of her grief subsided before the spectacle of sorrow everywhere. Ceasing to be occupied with its own selfish pang, her heart flowed out in strong yearnings of sympathy with the universal suffering. Her tears of anguish softened into tears of pity; her passion melted away in compassion. She forgot herself in the general interest and found redemption in redeeming.

5. *Do not chide yourself for feeling strongly.* Tears are natural. A thunderstorm without rain is fraught with peril; but the pattering raindrops cool the air and relieve the overcharged atmosphere. The swollen brooks indicate that the snows are melting on the hills and spring is near.

"Daughters of Jerusalem," said our Lord, " . . . weep for yourselves, and your children" (Luke 23:28). To bear sorrow with dry eyes and stolid heart may befit a Stoic but not a Christian. We have no need to rebuke fond nature crying for its mate, its lost joy, the touch of the vanished hand, or the sound of the voice that is still, provided only that the will is resigned. This is the one consideration for those who suffer. *Is the will right?* If it isn't, God Himself cannot comfort. If it is, then the path will inevitably lead from the valley of the shadow of death to the banqueting table and the overflowing cup.

Many say, "I cannot feel resigned. It is bad enough to have my grief to bear; but I have this added trouble, that I cannot *feel* resigned." My invariable reply is: "You probably never can feel resignation, but you can *will* it."

The Lord Jesus in the Garden of Gethsemane has shown us how to suffer. He chose His Father's will. Though Judas, prompted by Satan, was the instrument for mixing the cup and placing it to the Savior's lips, he looked right beyond Judas to the Father, who permitted him to work his cruel way. And He said: "The cup which my Father hath given me, shall I not drink it?" (John 18:11). And He said repeatedly, "If this cup may not pass away from me, except I drink it, thy will be done" (Matt. 26:42; cf. v. 39). He gave up His own way and will, saying, "I will Thy will, O My Father!"

117

Let all sufferers who read these lines go apart and dare to say the same words: "Your will, and not mine. Your will be done in the earth of my life, as in the heaven of Your purpose. I choose Your will." Say this thoughtfully and deliberately, not because you can feel it, but because you will it; not because the way of the cross is pleasant, but because it must be right. Say it repeatedly—whenever the surge of pain sweeps through you, whenever the wound begins to bleed afresh: "Not my will, but Thine be done." *Dare to say yes to God.* "Even so, Father: for so it seemed good in Thy sight" (Matt. 11:26).

And so you will be led to feel that all is right and well; and a great calm will settle down on your heart, a peace that "passeth all understanding" (Phil. 4:7)—a sense of rest, which is not inconsistent with suffering but walks in the midst of it as the three young men in the fiery furnace (Dan. 3), to whom the burning coals must have been like the dewy grass of a forest glade. As one person said, "The doctor told us our little child was dying. I felt like a stone. But *in a moment* I seemed to give up my hold on her. She appeared no longer mine, but God's."

6. *Be sure to learn God's lessons.* Each sorrow carries at its heart a germ of holy truth that, if you get and sow in the soil of your heart, will bear harvests of spiritual fruit, as seeds from mummy cases bear fruit in English soil. God has a meaning in each blow of His chisel, each incision of His knife. He knows the way that He takes. But His object is not always clear to us.

In suffering and sorrow God touches the minor chords and develops the passive virtues. He opens to view the treasures of darkness, the constellations of promise, the rainbow of hope, the silver light of the covenant. What is human character without sympathy, submission, patience, trust, and hope that grips the unseen truth as an anchor? But these graces are possible only through sorrow. Sorrow is a garden, the trees of which are laden with the peaceable fruits of righteousness; do not leave it without bringing them with you. Sorrow is a mine, the walls of which glisten with precious stones; do not retrace your steps into daylight without some specimens. Sorrow is a school. You are sent to sit on its hard benches and learn from its black-lettered pages the lessons that will make you wise forever; do not trifle away your chance of graduating there. No wonder Frances Havergal used to talk of "turned-in lessons" at the school of life!

7. *Count on the joys afterward.* God will not always be causing grief. He traverses the dull brown acres with His plow, seaming the yielding earth, so that He may be able to cast in the precious grain. Believe that in days of sorrow He is sowing light for the righteous and gladness for the upright in heart. Look forward to the reaping. Anticipate the joy that is set before you, which shall flood your heart with minstrel notes when patience has had her perfect work.

You will live to recognize the wisdom of God's choice for you. You will one day see that the thing you wanted was only second best. You will be surprised to remember that you once nearly broke your heart and spilled the wine of your life for what would never have satisfied you, if you had caught it, as the child the butterfly or soap bubble. You will meet again your beloved. You will have again your love. You will become possessed of a depth of character, a breadth of sympathy, a fund of patience, an ability to understand and help others, which, as you lay them at Christ's feet for him to use, will make you glad that you were afflicted. You will see God's plan and purpose; you will reap His harvest; you will behold His face and be satisfied. Each wound will have its pearl; each carcass will contain a swarm of bees; each foe, like Midian to Gideon, will yield its goodly spoil.

The way of the cross, rightly borne, is the only way to the everlasting light of God. The path that threads the Garden of Gethsemane and climbs over the hill of Calvary alone conducts us to the visions of the Easter morning and the glories of the Ascension mount. If we will not drink of His cup, be baptized with His baptism, or take our fill of that which is behind His sufferings, we cannot expect to share in the joy of His espousals and the ecstasy of His triumph. But if these conditions are fulfilled, we will not miss one note in the everlasting song, one element of the bliss that is possible to men.

8. *Remember that somehow suffering, rightly borne, enriches and helps mankind.* The death of Hallam was the birthday of Tennyson's *In Memoriam.* The cloud of insanity that brooded over Cowper gave us "God Moves in a Mysterious Way." Milton's blunders taught him to sing of "Holy Light, offspring of heaven firstborn." Rist used to say, "The dear cross has pressed many songs out of me." And it is probable that none rightly suffer anywhere without contributing something to the alleviation of human grief and to the triumph of good over evil, of love over hate, and of light over darkness.

If you believed this, could you not bear to suffer? Is not the chief misery of all suffering its loneliness and perhaps its apparent aimlessness? Then dare to believe that no man dies to himself. Fall to the ground bravely and cheerfully to die. If you refuse this, you will abide alone; but if you yield to it, you will bear fruit that will sweeten the lot of mankind and strengthen the life of others who will never know your name or stop to thank you for your help.

Human life is becoming richer as the generations pass, because each contributes its special ingredient to the general sum of good. The leaves fall unnoticed on the forest floor and rot, but the soil grows richer. All suffering rightly borne fills up that which is behind the sufferings of Christ and helps (though it has no substitutionary value) to hasten the redemptive processes that work out from His cross.

THE SECRET
OF GUIDANCE

THE SECRET
OF GUIDANCE

ANY children of God are so deeply exercised on the matter of guidance that it may be helpful to give a few suggestions about how to know the way in which our Father would have us walk and the work He would have us do. The importance of the subject cannot be exaggerated. So much of our power and peace consists in knowing where God would have us be and in being just there.

The manna only falls where the cloudy pillar of God broods; it is certain to be found on the sands that a few hours ago were glistening in the flashing light of the heavenly fire and are now shadowed by the fleecy canopy of cloud. If we are precisely where our heavenly Father would have us to be, we are perfectly sure that He will provide food, raiment, and everything beside. When He sends His servants to Cherith, He will make even the ravens to bring them food (1 Kings 17).

How much of our Christian work has been abortive because we have initiated it for ourselves instead of ascertaining what God was doing and where He required our presence. We dream bright dreams of success. We try to command it. We call to our aid all kinds of expedients, questionable or otherwise. And at last we turn back, disheartened and ashamed, like children who are torn and scratched by the brambles and soiled by the quagmire. None of this had come about, if only we had been from the first under God's unerring guidance. He might test us, but He could not allow us to mistake His will.

SEEKING GUIDANCE

Naturally, the child of God longing to know his Father's will turns to the sacred Book and refreshes his confidence by noticing how in all ages God has guided those who dared to trust Him up to the very hilt, though at the time they must have been as perplexed as we are often now. We know how Abraham left kindred and country and started, with no other guide than God, across the trackless desert to a land that he knew not. We know how the Israelites were led for forty years through the peninsula of Sinai, with its labyrinths of red sandstone and its wastes of sand. We know how Joshua, in entering the Land of Promise, was able to cope with the difficulties of an unknown region and overcome great and warlike nations because he looked to the Captain of the Lord's host, who ever leads to victory. We know how, in the early church, the apostles were enabled to thread their way through the most difficult questions and solve the most perplexing problems; they laid down principles that will guide the church to the end of time because the Holy Spirit revealed to them what they should do and say.

The promises of guidance are unmistakable. Psalm 32:8 says, "I will instruct thee and teach thee in the way which thou shalt go: I will guide thee with mine eye." This is God's distinct assurance to those whose transgressions are forgiven, whose sins are covered, and who are more quick to notice the least symptom of His will than a horse or mule to feel the bit.

Proverbs 3:6 declares, "In all thy ways acknowledge him, and he shall direct [make plain] thy paths." This is a sure word on which we may rest, if only we fulfill the previous conditions of trusting God with all our heart and not leaning to our own understanding (v. 5).

Isaiah 58:11 says, "The LORD shall guide thee continually." It is impossible to think that He could guide us at all if He did not guide us always. The greatest events of life, like the huge rocking stones in the west of England, revolve on the smallest points. A pebble may alter the flow of a stream. The growth of a grain of mustard seed may determine the rainfall of a continent. Thus, we are bidden to look for a guidance that will embrace the whole of life in all its myriad necessities.

In John 8:12, Jesus affirms, "I am the light of the world: he that followeth me shall not walk in darkness, but shall have the light of life." The reference to "darkness" here seems to be to the wilderness wanderings; and the Master promises to be to all faithful souls, in their pilgrimage to the City of God, what the cloudy pillar was to the children of Israel on their march to the Land of Promise.

These are but specimens of God's promise. The vault of Scripture is inlaid with thousands such as these, which glisten in their measure as the stars that guide the wanderer across the deep.

And yet it may appear to some tried and timid hearts as if every person mentioned in the Word of God was helped, but they are left without help. They seem to have stood before perplexing problems, face to face with life's mysteries, eagerly longing to know what to do; but no angel has come to tell them, and no iron gate has opened to free them from the prisonhouse of circumstances.

Some lay the blame on their own stupidity. Their minds are blunt and dull. They cannot catch God's meaning, which would be clear to others. They are so nervous of doing wrong that they cannot learn clearly what is right. Yet how do we treat our children? One child is so bright-witted and so keen that a little hint is enough to indicate the way; another was born dull and cannot take in your meaning quickly. Do you only let the clever one know what you want? Will you not take the other upon your knee and make clear to it the directions that are baffling? Does not the distress of the tiny nursling, who longs to know that it may immediately obey, weave an almost stronger bond than that which binds you to the rest? O weary, perplexed, and stupid children, believe in the great love of God and cast yourselves upon it, sure that He will come down to your ignorance and suit Himself to your needs. He will take "the lambs with his arm, and carry them in his bosom, and shall *gently lead* those that are with young" (Isa. 40:11, italics added).

HOW TO HEED
GOD'S DIRECTIONS

There are certain practical directions that we must heed in order to be led into the mind of the Lord:

1. *Your motives must be pure.* "When thine eye is single, thy whole body also is full of light" (Luke 11:34). You have been much in darkness lately, and perhaps this passage will point the reason. Your eye has not been "single." There has been some obliquity of vision, a spiritual squint, and this has hindered you from discerning indications of God's will that otherwise would have been as clear as noonday.

We must be very careful in judging our motives. We must search them as the detectives at the doors of the House of Commons search each stranger who enters. When by the grace of God we have been delivered from more gross forms of sin, we are still liable to the subtle working of self in our holiest and loveliest hours. It poisons our motives. It breathes decay on our fairest fruit-bearing. It whispers seductive flatteries into our pleased ears. It turns the spirit from its holy purpose, as the masses of iron on ocean steamers deflect the needle of the compass from the pole.

So long as there is some thought of personal advantage, some idea of acquiring the praise and commendation of men, some aim at self-aggrandizement, it will be simply impossible to find out God's purpose concerning us. The door must be resolutely shut against all this, if we would hear the still small voice. All crosslights must be excluded if we would see the Urim and Thummim stone brighten with God's yes or darken with His no.

Ask the Holy Spirit to give you the single eye and to inspire in your heart one aim alone—that which animated our Lord and enabled Him to cry, as He reviewed His life, "I have glorified thee on the earth" (John 17:4). Let this be the watchword of our lives,

"Glory to God in the highest" (Luke 2:14). Then our "whole body therefore [shall] be full of light, having no part dark, . . . as when the bright shining of a candle doth give thee light" (Luke 11:36).

2. *Your will must be surrendered.* "My judgment is just; because I seek not mine own will, but the will of the Father which hath sent me" (John 5:30). This was the secret that Jesus not only practiced but taught. In one form or another He was constantly insisting on a surrendered will, as the key to perfect knowledge, "If any man will do his will, he shall know . . . " (John 7:17a).

There is a great difference between a will that is extinguished and one that is surrendered. God does not demand that our wills should be crushed out, like the sinews of a fakir's unused arm. He only asks that they should say yes to Him. He expects us to become pliant to Him, as the willow twig to the practiced hand of the gardener.

On many occasions, as an ocean steamer has neared the quay, have I watched a little lad take his place beneath the poop with his eye and ear fixed on the captain, waiting to shout each word he utters to the grimy engineers below. Often have I longed that my will should repeat as accurately and as promptly the words and will of God, so that all my lower nature might obey.

It is for the lack of this subordination that we so often miss the guidance we seek. There is a secret controversy between our will and God's. And we will never be right till we have let Him take, break, and make our will His. Oh, do seek that! If you cannot give your will, let Him take it. If you are not willing, confess that you are willing to be made willing. Hand yourself over to let Him will and do of His own good pleasure. We must be as plastic clay, ready to take any shape that the great potter may choose, so will we be able to detect His guidance.

3. *Seek information for your mind.* This is certainly the next step. God has given us these wonderful faculties of brain power, and He will not ignore them. In the days of the Reformation He did not destroy the Roman Catholic churches or pulpits; He did better—he preached in them. And in grace he does not cancel the action of any of His marvelous bestowments, but he uses them for the communication of His purposes and thoughts.

It is of the greatest importance, then, that we should feed our minds with facts, with reliable information, with the results of human experience, and above all with the teachings of the Word of God. It is matter for the utmost admiration to notice how full the Bible is of biography and history, so that there is hardly a single crisis in our lives that may not be matched from those wondrous pages. There is no book like the Bible for casting a light on the dark landings of human life.

We have no need or right to run hither and thither to ask our friends what we ought to do. But there is no harm in our taking pains to gather all reliable information on which the flame of holy thought and consecrated purpose may feed and grow strong. It is for us ultimately to decide as God will teach us; but His voice may come to us through the voice of sanctified common sense, acting on the materials we have collected. Of course, at times God may bid us act against our reason, but these are very exceptional; and then our duty will be so clear that there can be no mistake. For the most part, God will speak in the results of deliberate consideration, weighing and balancing the pros and cons.

When Peter was shut up in prison and could not possibly extricate himself, an angel was sent to do for him what he could not do for himself; but when they had passed through a street or two of the city, the angel left him to consider the matter for himself. Thus God treats us still. He will dictate a miraculous course by miraculous methods. But when the ordinary light of reason is adequate to the task, He will leave us to act as occasion may serve.

4. *Be much in prayer for guidance.* The Psalms are full of earnest pleadings for clear direction, such as this: "Teach me thy way, O LORD, and lead me in a plain path, because of mine enemies" (Ps. 27:11). Furthermore, it is the law of our Father's house that His children will ask for what they want. "If any of you lack wisdom, let him ask of God, that giveth to all men liberally, and upbraideth not" (James 1:5).

In a time of change and crisis, we need to be much in prayer, not only on our knees but in that sweet form of inward prayer in which the spirit is constantly offering itself up to God, asking to be shown His will. In such inward prayer, the human spirit is soliciting that it may be impressed upon its surface, as the heavenly bodies photograph themselves on prepared paper. Wrapped in prayer like this, the trustful believer may tread the deck of the ocean steamer night after night, sure that He who points the stars their courses will not fail to direct the soul that has no other aim than to do His will.

One good form of prayer at such a juncture is to ask that doors may be shut, that the way may be closed, and that all enterprises that are not according to God's will may be arrested at their very beginning. Put the matter absolutely into God's hands from the outset, and He will not fail to shatter the project and defeat the aim that is not according to His holy will.

5. *Await the gradual unfolding of God's plan in providence.* God's impressions upon our spirits within and through His Word without are always corroborated by His providence around, and we should quietly wait until these three focus into one point.

Sometimes it looks as if we are bound to act. Every one says we must do something; and indeed things seem to have reached so desperate a pitch that we must. Behind us are Egyptians; right and left are inaccessible precipices; before is the sea. It is not easy at such times to "stand still, and see the salvation of the LORD" (Exod. 14:13); but we must. When Saul compelled himself to offer sacrifice because he thought that Samuel was too late in coming, he made the great mistake of his life (1 Sam. 13).

God may delay to come in the guise of His providence. There was delay before Sennacherib's host lay like withered leaves around the Holy City. There was delay before Jesus came walking on the sea in the early dawn or hastened to raise Lazarus. There was delay before the angel sped to Peter's side on the night before his expected martyrdom. He stays long enough to test the patience of our faith, yet not a moment behind the extreme hour of need. We should remember God's warning to the prophet: "The vision is yet for an appointed time, but at the end it shall speak, and not lie: though it tarry, wait for it; because it will surely come, it will not tarry" (Hab. 2:3).

It is very remarkable how God guides us by circumstances. At one moment the way may seem utterly blocked; and then shortly afterward some trivial incident occurs that might not seem much to others but which to the keen eye of faith speaks volumes. Sometimes these signs are repeated in different ways in answer to prayer. They are not haphazard results of chance but the opening up of circumstances in the direction in which we should walk. And they begin to multiply as we advance toward our goal, just as lights do as we near a populous town, when darting through the land by night express.

Sometimes men sigh for an angel to come to point them their way; that simply indicates that as yet the time has not come for them to move. If you do not know what you ought to do, stand still until you do. And when the time comes for action, circumstances will sparkle like glowworms along your path. You will become so sure that you are right when God's three witnesses concur (the inward impression, the outward Word, the surrounding circumstances) that you could not be surer, though an angel beckoned you on.

The circumstances of our daily life are to us an infallible indication of God's will, when they concur with the inward promptings of the Spirit and with the Word of God. So long as they are stationary, wait. When you must act, they will open, and a way will be made through oceans and rivers, wastes and rocks.

GUARANTEED GUIDANCE
AS GOD ORDAINS

We often make a great mistake by thinking that God is not guiding us at all because we cannot see far in front. But this is not His method. He only assures us that *the steps* of a good man should be ordered by the

Lord (Ps. 37:23). Not guidance for next year, but for tomorrow. Not for the next mile, but the next yard. Not the whole pattern, but the next stitch in the canvas. If you expect more than this, you will be disappointed and stumble back into the dark. But the proper expectation will secure for you leading in the right way, as you will acknowledge when you review it from the hilltops of glory.

We cannot ponder too deeply the lessons of the cloud given in the exquisite picture lesson of guidance (Num. 9:15–23). Let us look high enough for guidance. Let us encourage our soul to wait only upon God till it is given. Let us cultivate that meekness that He will guide in judgment. Let us seek to be of quick understanding that we may be apt to see the least sign of His will. Let us stand with girded loins and lighted lamps so that we may be prompt to obey. Blessed are those servants. They will be led by a right way to the golden city of the saints.

Speaking for myself, after months of waiting and prayer, I have become absolutely sure of the guidance of my heavenly Father; and with the emphasis of personal experience, I would encourage each troubled and perplexed soul that may read these lines to wait patiently for the Lord until He clearly indicates His will.

The waiting is not always on our side alone. God also waits. He waits to be gracious—waits until we have learned the lesson He dare not allow us to miss, waits until we have taken the position in which He can bless us without injury. He holds back blessings that will enrich your life with new meaning and beauty until you have done your full part in the preparation of the soil and the casting in of the seed.

WHERE AM I
WRONG?

WHERE AM I WRONG?

HIS is your eager question, O Christian soul, and your bitter complaint. On the faces and in the lives of others you have discerned a light, a joy, a power that you envy with a desire that oppresses you, but for which you should thank God devoutly. It is well when we are dissatisfied with the low levels on which we have been wont to live, and begin to ask the secret of a sweeter, nobler, more victorious life. The sleeper who turns restlessly is near awakening and will find that already the light of the morning is shining around the couch on which slumber has been indulged too long. "Awake, thou that sleepest, and arise from the dead, and Christ shall give thee light" (Eph. 5:14).

PARTIAL EXPLANATIONS

1. *We must, however, remember that temperaments differ.* Some seem born in the dark and carry with them through life a hereditary predisposition to melancholy.

Their nature is set to a minor key and responds most easily and naturally to depression. They look always on the dark side of things, and in the bluest of skies they discover the cloud no bigger than a man's hand. Theirs is a shadowed pathway, where glints of sunshine strike feebly and with difficulty through the dark foliage above.

Such a temperament may be yours; and if it is, you never can expect to obtain the same exuberant gladness that comes to others, nor must you complain if that is so. This is the burden your Savior's hands shaped for you; and you must carry it for Him, not complaining or parading it to the gaze of others or allowing it to master your steadfast and resolute spirit, but bearing it silently and glorifying God amid all. Though it may be impossible for you to win the joyousness that comes to others, there may at least be rest, and victory, and serenity—heaven's best gift to mankind.

2. *We must remember also that emotion is no true test of our spiritual state.* Rightness of heart often shows itself in gladness of heart, just as bodily health generally reveals itself in exuberant spirits. But it is not always so. In other words, absence of joy does not always prove that the heart is wrong. It may do so, but not invariably. The nervous system may have been overtaxed, as Elijah's was in the wilderness when, after the long strain of Carmel and his flight was over, he lay down upon the sand and asked to die—a request that God met, not with rebuke, but with food and sleep (1 Kings 19). Perhaps the Lord has withdrawn the light from the landscape in order to see whether He is loved for Himself or merely for His gifts. Perhaps the discipline of life has culminated in a Gethsemane where the bitter cup is being placed to the lips by a Father's hand,

though only a Judas can be seen; and in the momentary anguish caused by the effort to renounce the will, it is only possible to lie upon the ground with strong crying and tears, which the night wind bears to God. Under such circumstances as these, exuberant joy is out of place. Somber colors become the tried and suffering soul. High spirits would be as unbecoming here as gaiety in the home shadowed by death. Patience, courage, faith are the suitable graces to be manifested at such times.

BASIC REASONS

But when allowance is made for all these, it is certain that many of us are culpably missing a blessedness that would make us radiant with the light of paradise; and the loss is attributable to some defect in character, which we will do well to detect and make right.

1. *Perhaps you do not distinguish between your standing and your experience.* Our experiences are as fickle as April weather—now sunshine, now cloud; lights and shadows chasing each other over miles of heathery moor or foam-flecked sea. But our standing in Jesus changes not. It is like Jesus Himself: the same yesterday, today, and forever. It did not originate in us but in His everlasting love, which, foreseeing all that we should be, loved us notwithstanding all. It has not been purchased by us but by His precious blood, which pleads for us as mightily and successfully when we can hardly claim it as when our faith is most buoyant. It is not maintained by us but by the Holy Spirit. If we have fled to Jesus for salvation—sheltering under Him, relying on Him, and trusting Him, though with many

misgivings, as well we may—then we are one with Him forever. We were one with Him in the grave, one with Him on Easter morn, one with Him when He sat down at God's right hand. We are one with Him now as He stands in the light of his Father's smile, just as the limbs of the swimmer are one with the head, though it alone is encircled with the warm glory of the sun while they are hidden beneath the waves. No doubt or depression can for a single moment affect or alter our acceptance with God through the blood of Jesus, which is an eternal fact.

You have not realized this, perhaps, but have thought that your standing in Jesus was affected by your changeful mood, as might the fortune of a ward in chancery be diminished or increased by the amount of her spending money. Our standing in Jesus is our invested capital, while our emotions are but our spending money, which is ever passing through our pocket or purse, never exactly the same. Cease to consider how you feel and build on the immovable rock of what Jesus is, and has done, and is doing, and will do for you, world without end.

2. *Perhaps you live too much in your feelings, too little in your will.* We have no direct control over our feelings, but we have control over our wills. As the hymn writer declares, "Our wills are ours, to make them Thine." God hold us responsible, not for what we *feel,* but for what we *will.* In His sight we are not what we feel but what we will. Let us therefore not live in the summer house of emotion, but in the central citadel of the will, wholly yielded and devoted to the will of God.

At the Table of the Lord the soul is often suffused with holy emotion; the tides rise high, the tumultuous torrents of joy knock loudly against the floodgates as if to beat them down, and every element in the nature joins in the choral hymn of rapturous praise. But the morrow comes, and life has to be faced in the grimy counting house, the dingy shop, the noisy factory, the godless workroom; and as the soul compares the joy of yesterday with the difficulty experienced in walking humbly with the Lord, it is inclined to question whether it is quite so devoted and consecrated as it was. But at such a time how fair a thing it is to remark that the will has not altered its position by a hair's breadth. At that moment one should look up and say, "My God, the tide of emotion has passed away like a summer brook; but You know I am as devoted, as loyal, as desirous to be only for You, as in the blessed moment of unbroken retirement at Your feet." This is an offering with which God is well pleased. And thus we may live a calm, peaceful life.

3. *Perhaps you have disobeyed some clear command.* Sometimes a soul comes to its spiritual adviser, speaking thus: "I have no conscious joy and have had but little for years."

"Did you once have it?"

"Yes, for some time after my conversion to God."

"Are you conscious of having refused obedience to some distinct command that came into your life but from which you shrank?"

Then the face is cast down, and the eyes film with tears, and the answer comes with difficulty.

"Yes, years ago I used to think that God required a certain thing of me; but I felt I could not do what He wished. I was uneasy for some time about it, but after a while it seemed to fade from my mind, and now it does not often trouble me."

"Ah, friend, that is where you have gone wrong. And you will never get right till you go back through the weary years to the point where you dropped the thread of obedience and perform that one thing that God demanded of you so long ago but on account of which you did leave the narrow track of implicit obedience."

Is not this the cause of depression to thousands of Christian people? They are God's children, but they are disobedient children. The Bible rings with one long demand for obedience. The key words of the Book of Deuteronomy are *observe* and *do*. The burden of the Farewell Discourse is, "If ye love me, keep my commandments" (John 14:15). We must not question or reply or excuse ourselves. We must not pick and choose our way. We must not take some commands and reject others. We must not think that obedience in other directions will compensate for disobedience in some particular. God gives one command at a time, borne in upon us, not in one way only but in many; by this He tests us. If we obey in this, He will flood our soul with blessing and lead us forward into new paths and pastures. But if we refuse in this, we will remain stagnant and waterlogged, make no progress in Christian experience, and lack both power and joy.

4. *Perhaps you are permitting some known evil.* When water is left to stand, the particles of silt betray themselves as they fall one by one to the bottom. So, if you are quiet, you may become aware of the presence in your soul of permitted evil. Dare to consider it. Do not avoid the sight, as the bankrupt who avoids his telltale ledgers or as the consumptive patient the stethoscope. Compel yourself to consider quietly whatever evil the Spirit of God discovers to your soul. It

may have lurked in the cupboards and cloisters of your being for years, suspected but unjudged. But whatever it be and whatever its history, it has brought the shadow over your life, which is your daily sorrow.

Does your will refuse to relinquish a practice or habit that is alien to the will of God?

Do you permit some secret sin to have its unhindered way in the house of your life?

Do your affections roam unrestrained after forbidden objects?

Do you cherish any resentment or hatred towards another, to whom you refuse to be reconciled?

Is there some injustice that you refuse to forgive, some charge that you refuse to pay, some wrong that you refuse to confess?

Are you allowing something in yourself that you would be the first to condemn in others but that you argue may be permitted in your own case because of certain reasons with which you attempt to smother the remonstrances of conscience?

In some cases the hindrance to conscious blessedness lies not in sins, but in *weights* that hang around the soul. Sin is that which is always and everywhere wrong; but a weight is anything that may hinder or impede the Christian life without being positively sin. Thus, a thing may be a weight to one but not so to another. "Let every man be fully persuaded in his own mind" (Rom. 14:5). And wherever the soul is aware that its life is hindered by the presence of only one thing, then however harmless in itself and however innocently permitted by others, there can be no alternative, but it must be cast aside—as the garments of the lads when on the village green they compete for the prize of the wrestle or the race.

5. *Perhaps you look too much inwards on self, instead of outwards on the Lord Jesus.* The healthiest people do not think about their health, while the weak induce disease by morbid introspection. If you begin to count your heartbeats, you will disturb the rhythmic action of the heart. If you continually imagine a pain anywhere, you will produce it. Likewise some true children of God induce their own darkness by morbid self-scrutiny. They are always going back on themselves, analyzing their motives, reconsidering past acts of consecration, comparing themselves with themselves. In one form or another, self is the pivot of their lives, even though they undoubtedly live a religious life. What but darkness can result from such a course? There certainly are times in our lives when we must look within and judge ourselves, so that we may not be judged. But this is only done that we may turn with fuller purpose of heart to the Lord. And when once done, it needs not to be repeated. "Forgetting those things which are behind" (Phil. 3:13) is the only safe motto. The question is not whether we did as well as we might but whether we did as well as we could at the time.

We must spend our lives, not in cleaning our windows or in considering whether they are clean, but in sunning ourselves in God's blessed light. That light will soon show us what still needs to be cleansed away and will enable us to cleanse it with unerring accuracy. Our Lord Jesus is a perfect reservoir of everything the soul of man requires for a blessed and holy life. To make much of Him, to abide in Him, to draw from Him, to receive each moment from His fullness, is therefore the only condition of soul health. But to be more concerned with self than with Him is like spending much time and thought over the senses of the body, never using them for the purpose of receiving impressions from the world outside. Look unto Jesus. "Delight thyself also in the Lord" (Ps. 37:4). "My soul, wait thou only upon God" (Ps. 62:5).

6. *Perhaps you spend too little time in communion with God through His Word.* It is not necessary to make long prayers; but it is essential to be much alone with God, waiting at His door, hearkening for His voice, lingering in the garden of Scripture for the coming of the Lord God in the dawn or cool of the day. No number of meetings, no fellowship with Christian friends, no amount of Christian activity can compensate for the neglect of the still hour.

When you feel least inclined for it, there is most need to make for your closet with the shut door. Do for duty's sake what you cannot do as a pleasure, and you will find it becomes delightful. You can better thrive without nourishment than become happy or strong in Christian life without fellowship with God.

When you cannot pray for yourself, begin to pray for others. When your desires flag, take the Bible in hand and begin to turn each text into petition; or take up the tale of your mercies and begin to translate each of them into praise. When the Bible itself becomes irksome, inquire whether you have not been spoiling your appetite by sweetmeats and renounce them. Believe that the Word is the wire along which the voice of God will certainly come to you, if the heart is hushed and the attention fixed. "I will hear what God the LORD will speak" (Ps. 85:8).

More Christians than we can count are suffering from a lack of prayer and Bible study, and no revival is more to be desired than that of systematic private Bible study. No short and easy method of godliness can dispense with this.

Many also suffer from the spirit of organization and routine, which is so rife in Christian work. We do so much; and we do it mechanically. We are wheels in the great machinery instead of souls, the value of whose work in the world depends much more on what they are than on what they say or do. We must keep fresh, tender, unselfish, and devout. And it were better to relinquish some of the routine of life than lose the temper and tone of heart, which are all important for the redemption of others.

7. *Perhaps you have never given yourself entirely over to the mastership of the Lord Jesus.* We are His by many ties and rights, but too few of us recognize His lordship. We are willing enough to take Him as Savior; but we hesitate to make Him King. We forget that God has exalted Him to be Prince as well as Savior, yet the divine order is irreversible. Those who ignore the lordship of Jesus cannot build up a strong or happy life.

Put the sun in its central throne, and all the motions of the planets assume a beautiful order. Put Jesus on the throne of the life, and all things fall into harmony and peace. Seek first the kingdom of God, and all things are yours (Matt. 6:33). Consecration is the indispensable condition of blessedness.

So shall light break on your path, such as has not shone there for many days. Yes, "thy sun shall no more go down; neither shall thy moon withdraw itself: for the LORD shall be thine everlasting light, *and the days of thy mourning shall be ended*" (Isa. 60:20, italics added).

THE FIRST STEP
INTO THE BLESSED
LIFE

THE FIRST STEP
INTO THE BLESSED LIFE

HERE is a Christian life that, in comparison with that experienced by the majority of Christians, is a summer to winter or as the mature fruit of a golden autumn to the struggling promise of a cold, late spring. It is such a life as Caleb might have lived in Hebron, the city of fellowship, or the apostle John might have lived when he wrote his epistles. It may be fitly termed

THE BLESSED LIFE.

And the blessedness of the blessed life lies in this: that we trust the Lord to do in us and for us what we cannot do, and that we find He does not belie His Word but that, according to our faith, so it is done to us. The weary spirit that has vainly sought to realize its ideal by its own strivings and efforts now gives itself over to the strong and tender hands of the Lord Jesus; He accepts the task and at once begins to work in that life "to will and to do of his own good pleasure" (Phil. 2:13), delivering it from the tyranny of besetting sin and fulfilling in it His own perfect ideal.

This blessed life should be the normal life of every Christian—in work and rest, in the building up of the inner life, and in the working out of one's life plan. It is God's thought, not for a few, but for all of His children. The youngest and weakest may lay claim to it equally with the strongest and oldest. We should step into it at the moment of conversion, without wandering with blistered feet for forty years in the desert or lying for thirty-eight years, with disappointed hopes, in the porch of the House of Mercy (Bethesda).

But since many Christians have long ago passed the moment of conversion without entering the blessed life, it may be well to show clearly what the first step must be, to take us within its golden circle. Better to take it late than never. The first step into the blessed life is contained in one word—

CONSECRATION.

And it is enforced by the significant exhortation of the apostle Paul, "Neither yield ye your members as instruments of unrighteousness unto sin: but yield yourselves unto God, as those that are alive from the dead, and your members as instruments of righteousness unto God" (Rom. 6:13).

It is not enough to give our time or energy or money to God. Many will gladly give Him anything but *themselves*. But none of these things will be accounted a sufficient substitute by Him who gave, not only His possessions, but His very life for us. As the Lord Jesus was all for us, He asks that we should be all for Him—body, soul, and spirit—one reasonable service and gift.

That consecration is the stepping stone to blessedness is clearly established in the experience of God's children. For instance, Frances Ridley Havergal has left for us this record: "It was on Advent Sunday, December 1873, that I first saw clearly the blessedness of true consecration. I saw it as a flash of electric light, and what you see you can never unsee. *There must be full surrender before there can be full blessedness. God admits you by one into the other.* First I was shown that the body of Jesus Christ, His Son, cleanseth me from all sin; and then it was made plain to me that He who had thus cleansed me had power to keep me clean; *so I utterly yielded myself to Him and utterly trusted Him to keep me."* George Whitefield, the Wesley brothers, the great Welsh preacher Christmas Evans, the French pastor Jean Frederic Oberlin, and many more have given the same testimony. And in their mouths this truth may surely be regarded as established, that we must pass through Gilgal to the Land of Rest; that the straight gate of consecration alone leads into the blessed life.

1. *The ground of consecration is in the great Scripture statement that we are Christ's.* There is a twofold ground of His proprietorship: *We are His by purchase.* "Ye are not your own. . . . For ye are bought with a price" (1 Cor. 6:19–20). Step into that slave market where men and women are waiting like chattel to be bought. Yonder comes a wealthy planter who, after due examination, lays down his money for a number of men and women to stock his estate. From that moment, those persons are absolutely his property, as much so as his cattle or his sheep. All they possess, all they earn, is absolutely his. So the apostles reasoned

they were Christ's; often they began their epistles by calling themselves "the slaves of Jesus Christ." Paul went so far as to say that he bore in his body the branding marks of Jesus (Gal. 6:17). And are not all Christians Christ's, whether they live up to it or not, because He purchased them by His most precious blood? Second, *we are His by deed of gift*. The Father has given to the Son all who will come to him. If ever you have come, or will come, to Jesus Christ as your Savior, you show that you have been included in that wonderful donation (John 6:37). And is it likely that God gave only a part of us? No, as utterly as He gave His Son for us, so He has given us to His Son. And our Lord Jesus thinks much of that solemn transaction—though we often live as if it had never taken place, as if we were free to live as we pleased.

2. *The act of consecration is to recognize Christ's ownership, and to say with the whole heart, "Lord, I am Yours by right, and I wish to be Yours by choice."* The mighty men of Israel were willing to swim the rivers at their flood to come to David, their uncrowned but God-appointed king. And when they met him, they cried, "Thine we are, David, and on thy side, thou son of Jesse" (1 Chron. 12:18). They were his because God had given them to him; but they could not rest content till they were his also by their glad choice. Why should we not say the same to Jesus Christ? "Lord Jesus, I am Yours by right. Forgive me that I have lived so long as if I were my own. Now I gladly recognize that You have a rightful claim on all I have and am. I want to live as Yours henceforth; and I do solemnly and at this hour give myself to You. Yours in life and death. Yours absolutely and forever."

Do not try to make a covenant with God, lest you

should break it and be discouraged. But quietly fall into your proper attitude as one who belongs to Christ. Take as your motto the noble confession, "Whose I am and whom I serve." Breathe the grand, old lines:

> *Just as I am, Thy love unknown*
> *Hath broken every barrier down;*
> *Now to be Thine, yea, Thine alone,*
> *O Lamb of God, I come! I come!*
> *—Charlotte Elliott*

3. *Consecration is not the act of our feelings, but of our will.* Do not try to make yourself feel anything. Do not try to make yourself fit or good or earnest enough for Christ. God is working in you, whether you feel it or not. He is giving you power, at this moment, to will and to do His good pleasure. Believe this and act upon it at once. Say, "Lord Jesus, I am willing to be Yours." Or if you cannot say as much as that, say, "Lord Jesus, I am willing to be made willing to be Yours forevermore."

Consecration is made possible when we give up our wills *about everything.* As soon as we come to the point of giving ourselves to God, we are almost certain to become aware of the presence of one thing (if not of more) out of harmony with His will. And while we feel able to surrender ourselves at all other points, here we exercise reserve. Every room and cupboard in the house, with the exception of this, can be thrown open to the new occupant. Every limb in the body, but one, is submitted to the practiced hand of the Good Physician. But that small reserve spoils the whole. To give ninety-nine parts and withhold the hundredth undoes the whole transaction. Jesus will have all or none. And He is wise. Who would live in a fever-stricken house, so long as one room was not exposed to disinfectants? Who would undertake a case so long as the patient refused to submit one part of his body to examination? Who would become responsible for a bankrupt person so long as one ledger book was kept back? The reason that so many fail to attain the blessed life is that there is some point in which they hold back from God and concerning which they prefer to have their own way and will rather than His. In this one thing they will not yield their wills and accept God's. And this one thing mars the whole, robs them of peace, and compels them to wander in a spiritual desert.

4. *If you cannot give all, ask the Lord Jesus to take all, especially that which seems so hard to give.* Many Christians have been helped by hearing it put thus. Tell them to *give,* and they shake their heads despondently. They are like the little child who told her mother that she had been trying to give her heart to Jesus "but it wouldn't go." But ask them if they are willing for Jesus to come into their hearts and take all, and they will joyfully assent.

Tennyson says, "Our wills are ours to make them Thine." But sometimes it seems impossible to shape them out so as to match every corner and angle of the will of God. What a relief it is at such a moment to hand the will over to Christ, telling Him that we are *willing to be made willing* to have His will in all things. At that moment we can ask Him to melt our stubborn waywardness, to fashion our wills upon His anvil, and to bring us into perfect accord with Himself.

5. *When you are willing that the Lord Jesus should take all, you must believe that He does take all.* He does not wait for us to free ourselves from evil habits or make

ourselves good or feel glad and happy. His one desire is that we should put our wills on His side in everything. When this is done, He instantly enters the surrendered heart and begins His blessed work of renovation and renewal. From the very moment of consecration, though it be done in much feebleness and with slender appreciation of its entire meaning, the spirit may begin to say with new emphasis, "I am His! I am His! Glory to God, I am His!" Directly the gift is laid on the altar and the divine fire falls on it.

Sometimes there is a rush of holy feeling. It was so with James Brained Taylor, who tells, "I felt that I needed something I did not possess. I desired it, not for my benefit only, but for that of the church and the world. I lifted up my heart that the blessing might descend. At this juncture I was delightfully conscious of giving up all to God. I was enabled to say in my heart, *Here, Lord—Take me. Take my whole soul and seal me Thine now, Thine forever. If Thou wilt, Thou canst make me clean.* Then there ensued such emotions as I never before experienced. All was calm and tranquil, and a heaven of love pervaded my soul. I had the witness of God's love to me, and of mine to Him. Shortly after, I was dissolved in tears of love and gratitude to our blessed Lord, who came as King and took possession of my heart."

It is very delightful when such emotions are given to us. But we must not look for them or depend on them. Our consecration may be accepted by God and may excite the liveliest joy in our Savior's heart, though we are filled with no answering ecstasy. We may know that the great transaction is done, without any glad outburst of song. We may even have to exercise faith against feeling, as we say many times each day, "I am

His." But the absence of feeling proves nothing. At night we must pillow our heads on the conviction that Jesus took what we gave at the moment of our giving it, and that He will keep that which was committed to Him against that day (2 Tim. 1:12).

6. *It is well to make the act of consecration a definite one in our spiritual history.* George Whitefield did it in the ordination service: "I can call heaven and earth to witness that, when the bishop laid his hand upon me, I gave myself up to be a martyr for Him who hung upon the cross for me. Known unto Him are all the future events and contingencies. I have thrown myself blindfolded and without reserve into His almighty hands."

Christmas Evans did it as he was climbing a lonely mountainous road toward Cader Idris: "I was weary of a cold heart toward Christ, and began to pray, and soon felt the fetters loosening. Tears flowed copiously and I was constrained to cry out for the gracious visits of God. Thus I resigned myself to Christ, body and soul, gifts and labors, all my life, every day and every hour that remained to me; and all my cares I committed to Christ."

Stephen Grellet did it in the woods: "The woods are there of lofty and large pines, and my mind being inwardly retired before the Lord, He was pleased so to reveal His love to me through His blessed Son, my Savior, that my fears were removed, my wounds healed, my mourning turned into joy; and He strengthened me to offer up myself freely to Him and to His service, for my whole life."

It matters little when and how we do it—whether by speech or in writing, whether alone or in company—but we must not be content with a general desire. We must come to a definite act, at a given moment in time, when we will gladly acknowledge and confess Christ's absolute ownership of all we are and have.

7. *When the act of consecration is once truly done, it need not be repeated.* We may review it with thankfulness. We may add some new codicils to it. We may learn how much more was involved in it than we ever dreamed. We may find new departments of our being constantly demanding to be included. But we cannot undo it and need never repeat it; and if we fall away from it, let us go at once to our merciful High Priest, confessing our sin and seeking His forgiveness and restoration.

8. *The advantages resulting from this act cannot be enumerated here.* They pass all counting. The first and best is the special filling by the Holy Spirit; and as He fills the heart, He drives before Him the evil things that had held possession there too long—just as mercury poured into a glass of water sinks to the bottom, expels the water, and takes its place. Directly we give ourselves to Christ and He seals us with His Spirit. Directly we present Him with a yielded nature, and He begins to fill it with the Holy Spirit. Let us not try to feel that it is so. Let us believe that it is so and reckon on God's faithfulness. Others will soon see a marked difference in us, though we do not realize it.

9. *All that we have to do is to maintain this attitude of full surrender, by the grace of the Holy Spirit.* Remember that Jesus Christ offered Himself to God *through the eternal Spirit,* and He waits to do as much for you. Ask Him to maintain you in this attitude and to maintain this attitude in you. Use regularly the means of meditation, private prayer, and Bible study. Seek forgiveness for any failure as soon as you are conscious of it, and ask to be restored. Practice the holy habit of the constant recollection of God. Do not be eager to

work for God, but let God work through you. Accept everything that happens to you as being permitted and, therefore, sent by the will of Him who loves you infinitely. And there will roll in upon you wave upon wave, tide upon tide, ocean on ocean of an experience fitly called the "blessed life," because it is full of the happiness of the ever-blessed God Himself.

YOUR CHOICE

Dear reader, will you not take this step? There will be no further difficulty about money, dress, amusements, or similar questions that perplex some. Your heart will be filled and satisfied with the true riches of heaven. As the willing slave of Jesus Christ, you will only seek to do the will of your great and gentle Master—to spend every coin as He directs, to act as His steward, to dress so as to give Him pleasure, to spend time only as He may approve, to do His will on earth, as it is in heaven. All this will become easy and delightful for you.

You are perhaps far from this at present. But it is all within your reach. Do not be afraid of Christ. He wants to take nothing from you, except that which you would give up at once if you could see, as clearly as He does, the harm that it is inflicting. He will ask of you nothing inconsistent with the most perfect fitness and tenderness. He will give you grace enough to perform every duty He may demand. His yoke is easy, and His burden is light (Matt. 11:30).

Blessed Spirit of God, by whom alone human words can be made to speak to the heart, deign to use these words to point many a longing soul to the first step into the blessed life—for the exceeding glory of the Lord Jesus and for the sake of a dying world. Amen.

A KESWICK
EXPERIENCE

the Father had entrusted to Him on my behalf. And as I turned to retrace my steps to the town, I dared to reckon that it was mine as never before.

On my way to take a farewell glimpse of the lake, it being about midnight, I came on a group of friends engaged in discussing the meetings of the day and the engrossing theme of how to receive the Pentecostal gift. They were full of holy ecstasy, in strong contrast to my own recent experience, and seemed astonished at the thought that the same breath of God had not elicited a similar rapturous response as it swept the chords of my heart.

We passed through the swing-gate and walked by the side of the church, rearing itself above us in somber silence, and came on the terrace from which we could see Derwentwater gleaming below at the foot of the encircling hills. The night clouds were sweeping over it, veiling the stars and descending at intervals in light showers of rain. So we drew two benches together and, gathering close, began to compare our experience.

All alike confessed their liability to alternations of feeling, and even relapse in the inner life, when the conditions of soul health were neglected; but they laid a considerable stress on emotion as the test of their spiritual condition, and especially on the consciousness of joy or power in attesting the reception of the Holy Spirit. They reckoned that they were filled of the Spirit, so far as they felt His strivings and workings within; whereas, as I had received Him without emotion, I might expect ever to retain and even enlarge the measure of His fullness, whether the songbirds of summer or the stillness of winter occupied my heart.

After we had gone round the little circle and everyone had recited the sacred inner story, a young businessman broke in thus: "Is there not a danger of fixing your attention too much on the Holy Spirit and His methods, and too little on Him whom the Spirit came to reveal and glorify? My experience of the Holy Spirit is that He reveals Christ. It is the one desire of my life that the Spirit should make the Lord real to me; then sin cannot tempt, or danger frighten, me. I am a businessman; and if I lose the sense of His presence for half an hour, I lock myself into my counting house and ask the Holy Spirit what I have done to grieve Him and cause Him to veil that radiance from my heart."

"That's it!" we all exclaimed. "It is more of Jesus that we need. The Spirit is come to bear witness of and glorify Him."

Then we bowed our heads, and under a strong impulse humbly claimed that we might so receive the Holy Spirit that, whatever our company or engagements or experiences, Jesus might increasingly become the dear companion and guide of our lives.

THE PENTECOSTAL DIFFERENCE

Are *you* living in the power of the Pentecostal gift of the Holy Spirit? His advent on the Day of Pentecost was a distinct historical event, as distinct and as definite as the advent of our Lord to Bethlehem. You are living in the enjoyment of the blessings resulting from the latter; are you living also in the full experience of those that have accrued from the former? If not, you are missing the distinctive mark of Christianity, which gives it a unique position among all the religions of the world.

The apostles believed in Christ and called Him Master and Lord before Pentecost. In doing so, they bore witness to the operation of the Holy Spirit in their hearts. He had been working in the hearts of men from the beginning. But there was an immense difference between what they were before the Day of Pentecost and what they became as soon as the Spirit had come. It is evidently possible, then, for a man to be a believer in Christ and even to own Him as Lord through the gracious work of the Holy Spirit; and yet he may miss the deeper experiences of which Pentecost was the sign and seal. Is this your case?

On which side of Pentecost are you living? Historically, no doubt, you live on the hither side of that great day; but experimentally and practically you may be living on the other. You are in the great light, but you don't see it; you are in a gold region, but you are none the richer for it. Before you stands an open door into the heart of divine knowledge and power, but you have never attempted to enter it. While thousands are living as though Jesus had never come, died, and risen, *you* are living much as you would have if the gift of Pentecost never had been bestowed. Think! Is there anything in your Christian life that would have been different if the hour of Pentecost had never struck?

If not, be sure that there is something in Christianity that you have never tasted. There is a dividend awaiting you under Christ's new testament that you have never claimed but that, if apprehended and appropriated, would make your life rich and fragrant as a garden in May.

Three forms of the Greek word for *filled* are used in the Acts of the Apostles to describe the filling of the Spirit. These connote various states of spiritual fullness, which have their counterparts still:

Filled: a sudden, decisive experience for a specific work (Acts 4:8).

Were being filled: the imperfect tense, as though the blessed process were always going on (Acts 13:52).

Full: the adjective, indicating a perpetual state (Acts 6:8).

HOW TO KNOW YOU HAVE BEEN FILLED BY THE SPIRIT

There are several tests by which you may know whether you have participated in that filling of the Holy Spirit that is characteristic of the Pentecostal gift. Among these are the following:

1. *A consciousness of the presence of Christ.* Charles H. Spurgeon said once that he never passed a single quarter of an hour in his waking moments without a distinct consciousness of the presence of the Lord. When the Spirit fills the heart, Jesus is vividly real and evidently near. What is He to you? Do you wake in the morning beneath His light touch and spend the hours with Him? Can you frequently look up from your work and perceive His face? Are you constantly seeking from Him power, grace, and direction? If He is but a fitful vision, you have not realized the first mark of the Pentecostal gift.

2. *Deliverance from the power of sin.* The Holy Spirit is like fire. As fire purges metal, so does He the human heart. When He is within the heart in power, the germs of spiritual contagion are rendered harmless. When the human spirit is filled with the Holy Spirit, it will be conscious of temptation and more keenly alive to its least approach than ever before; but temptation will have no fascination, no power. People talk much of a clean heart; it seems to me wiser and truer to speak of the Holy Spirit as the indweller and cleanser, whose presence is purity.

3. *Minute and direct guidance.* I am speaking of no mere vagary or impulse, but guidance—in harmony with the Word of God on the one hand and the drift or trend of circumstances on the other. We must be quieter before God to detect it. Dr. A. T. Pierson showed me in his study at Philadelphia an armchair with special associations. He had been comforting a brother minister, who had been confined to his bed for six months, by suggesting that perhaps God had been compelled to lay him aside in order to get an opportunity of saying things that in his busy life he was unable to receive. Then suddenly the thought occurred to him that he too was giving God but few opportunities of communicating His will. Dr. Pierson resolved that henceforth he would spend at least half an hour each night sitting before God when his family had retired and the house was still. He said that during those times of retirement he had been distinctly conscious that God spoke with him and told him His will. If you are not led by the Spirit, you can be sure that you are not filled by Him.

4. *Power in service.* There is a difference between the Spirit being *in* and *on* us; He is the same Spirit, though in two different manifestations of His grace. Some have the Spirit of God in them for character, for example, but they are not gifted by Him for service. Our Lord Jesus, though conceived of the Holy Spirit, stood beneath the open heavens to be anointed of the Spirit before He entered on His public ministry. The church was held back from her work of evangelizing the world until she had received the Pentecostal enduement of power. Yet how many Christians are attempting to do this work without this power!

When speaking on this theme in a recent students'

convention at Northfield, Mr. D. L. Moody was completely broken down, and choked with weeping as he confessed that he was deeply conscious of his lack of this special power. All of the students broke down too, and he asked them to give up the customary afternoon sports and to meet him in the neighboring woods, that they might together seek a fresh anointing for service.

Are you conscious of possessing this qualification for soul winning? If not, why not claim your share of the Pentecostal life from your divine trustee and representative?

AWARENESS OF THE SPIRIT'S PRESENCE

We often wish that we could have been among the favored group of Christians when the Day of Pentecost had fully come and they were all together in the Upper Room (Acts 2). We think that we should have heard the sound as of the rushing of a mighty wind and received on our brows the encircling flame, in our hearts the blessed filling. But in all likelihood, if we had been there in our present condition, the hurricane of blessing would have swept past, leaving us dry and insensible. On the other hand, if that Pentecostal group were living now they would detect as much of the Spirit's presence, they would be as conscious of the working of the Lord Jesus, they would find life as full of God, as in the days when the church age was young. Peter would still be filled with the Holy Spirit and speak; Paul would be caught up into the third heaven and need a "thorn" to counterbalance the splendor of the revelations; John would find doors opening into heaven amid the conditions of our modern life, not less than when the crashing of the Aegean Sea rose from the beach of Patmos.

A change, you say, is needed. But there need be no change in your circumstances, in the atmosphere, or in the environment of your life. There is as much of the Holy Spirit within your reach as was present on the Day of Pentecost. This is the age of Pentecost. He waits to fill you as He did the 120 gathered in the Upper Room. The miraculous gifts have passed away because they are no longer needed; they are replaced by evidences that were not possible in those early days. But the essence of the Pentecostal gift, the filling of the Spirit, is as possible today as ever. "The promise," said the apostle Peter, alluding to our Savior's words, "is unto . . . all that are afar off, even as many as the Lord our God shall call" (Acts 2:39; cf. 1:4).

But of what use is it to live in a very ocean of power and love, if we are unable to discern its presence or appropriate its marvelous properties? Of what use is it that the land of the Hottentots is as full of electricity as London is, if they cannot use its mighty energy? Of what use is it that the summer days are full of dews, and heat, and light, and other materials out of which peaches and nectarines are made, if there are no peach blossoms nestling on the boughs to use them? Of what use is it that the floor is covered with nourishing food, if the newborn babe who lies beside it is unconscious of its existence and incapable of assimilating it?

HOW TO OBTAIN
THE BLESSING OF PENTECOST

There is no need to sigh for the lost age of gold, since the King of all ages is here. Had you lived with Him in His earthy life, the benefit would have been infinitesimal apart from *appropriating faith;* but if you have that, though you see Him not, you may secure His choicest gifts. These conditions, however, must be fulfilled before you can exercise that faith and receive that supreme gift:

1. *Be careful that you desire the filling of the Holy Spirit only for the glory of God.* If you want it so that you may realize a certain experience, or attract people to yourself, or transform some difficulty into a stepping stone, you are likely to miss it. You must be set on the one purpose of magnifying the Lord Jesus in your body, whether by life or death. Ask that all inferior motives may be destroyed and that this may burn strong and clear within you.

2. *Be cleansed from all sin of which you may be conscious.* If you have grieved God by impurity, anger, or unkind judgments of others, seek His forgiveness, restoration, and cleansing. The cleansed heart is an essential condition of the Spirit's filling.

3. *Present yourself and your members to God.* There should be no reserve, no locked cupboards, no closed doors, no vault barricaded from sun and air by a great slab of stone. Open every door and window of your being to the Holy Spirit, and he will certainly come in, though you may not be aware of the moment or method of His entrance.

4. *Give time to prayerful meditation on the Word of God.* There is no better way of communing with God than to walk to and fro in your own room or in the open air, your Bible in hand, meditating on it and turning its precepts and promises into prayer. God walks in the glades of Scripture, as of old in those of paradise.

5. *Then by faith reverently and humbly take the Father's gift through Jesus Christ.* Let it be a definite

172

transaction. Ask for the filling of the Spirit in the measure of Pentecost. Dip your bucket deep into the brimming well and bring it back dripping with crystal drops. Reckon that God has answered your prayer and has granted the petition you made. Meet every suggestion of doubt by the decisive answer that God is faithful and must do as He has said. But specially dare to act in faith, going to the temptation in the desert or the ministry among men, assured that you have received all the equipment that you could possibly require.

Whenever you are conscious of losing the Spirit's power, when the exhaustion of service has been greater that the reception of fresh supplies, when some new avenue of ministry or freshly discovered talent or new department of your being has presented itself to you— go to the same source for a refilling, a recharging with spiritual power, a reanointing by the holy chrism.

The lives that change other lives resemble, not the shallow streamlet, but the full ocean heaving beneath the great arch of the sky, which sends its pulse along the beach and far up the inlets and creeks. May such a life be ours in depth, in breadth, and in everlasting strength, by our being filled with the fullness of God!